DO220253

BFI SILVER

Representing the very best in critical writing on films and film-makers, these beautifully presented new editions and reissues of classic titles from BFI Publishing feature new introductions by leading film critics or scholars. They assess the unique contribution of the work in question and its author to the field of film studies and to the wider public understanding of moving image culture.

ALSO AVAILABLE:
Godard
A Long Hard Look at 'Psycho'

Rouben Mamoulian
2nd Edition

Tom Milne

with a foreword by Geoff Andrew

A BFI book published by Palgrave Macmillan

This edition published in 2010 by
PALGRAVE MACMILLAN

on behalf of the

BRITISH FILM INSTITUTE
21 Stephen Street, London W1T 1LN
www.bfi.org.uk

There's more to discover about film and television through the BFI. Our world-renowned archive, cinemas, festivals, films, publications and learning resources are here to inspire you.

Palgrave Macmillan in the UK is an imprint of Macmillan Publishers Limited, registered in England, company number 785998, of Houndmills, Basingstoke, Hampshire RG21 6XS. Palgrave Macmillan in the US is a division of St Martin's Press LLC, 175 Fifth Avenue, New York, NY 10010. Palgrave Macmillan is the global academic imprint of the above companies and has companies and representatives throughout the world. Palgrave® and Macmillan® are registered trademarks in the United States, the United Kingdom, Europe and other countries.

Cover design: keenan
Cover image: *Silk Stockings* (Rouben Mamoulian, 1957), Loew's Incorporated/© Arthur Freed Productions
Images provided by BFI Stills, Posters and Designs
Designed by couch
Printed in China

This book is printed on paper suitable for recycling and made from fully managed and sustained forest sources. Logging, pulping and manufacturing processes are expected to conform to the environmental regulations of the country of origin.

British Library Cataloguing-in-Publication Data
A catalogue record for this book is available from the British Library

ISBN 978-1-84457-352-3 (pb)
ISBN 978-1-84457-353-0 (hb)

(*previous page*) Rouben Mamoulian on the set of *Song of Songs*

Contents

Foreword to the 2nd Edition

GEOFF ANDREW

'Let us now praise famous men ...'

In an ideal world, it would have been gratifying to begin this foreword with the oft-quoted exhortation above;[1] the sad truth, however, is that neither the subject of this book nor its author is as well known as he deserves to be. Both, undoubtedly, ought to be 'famous'; but today's movie culture is more than ever given over to the here and now and the next big thing rather than to the long view, so that many self-proclaimed film buffs now appear to believe that cinema began with Scorsese and Lucas, or even with Tarantino. In this amnesiac world, the respective achievements of Messrs Mamoulian and Milne are unfortunately in even greater need of appraisal than when the latter's book was originally written.

In Tom Milne's case, the situation, while no less regrettable, is perhaps unsurprising; after all, many people – film-makers included – are openly antipathetic to critics, and it's long been held in some quarters that the critical fraternity consists primarily of failed artists who parasitically feed off their creative superiors, all too often by describing the work in negative and therefore deleterious terms. (To this 'argument' – 'Those who *can* become film-makers; those who *can't* become critics' – we'll return later.) In Mamoulian's case, however, the relative obscurity of his various achievements is altogether more baffling. It's not just that his very name is unknown to all but a small fraction of the cinephile community, nor that the exact nature of his contributions to his films as director is poorly grasped or insufficiently appreciated. No; even more depressingly, most of his films are now seldom screened other than on television (and there, of course, never in prime-time slots) and rarely mentioned at all even in purportedly thorough articles and books about the cinema.

A particularly conspicuous example is *Song of Songs*. Many regard Marlene Dietrich – rightly, of course – as a major screen actress, and she's best known and celebrated both for the six films she made with Josef von Sternberg and for titles like *Desire, Knight Without Armour, A Foreign Affair, Stage Fright, Rancho Notorious, Witness for the Prosecution, Touch of Evil* and *Judgment at Nuremberg. Song of Songs*, however – which boasts one of Dietrich's best performances and is, as Tom Milne perceptively notes, especially interesting for the way it plays with and fleshes out the iconic elements of her appeal that had been highlighted in the Sternberg films – is rarely name-checked, let alone discussed in any detail, in assessments of her career. Is that neglect a consequence of Mamoulian being less well known than Lubitsch, Clair, Wilder, Hitchcock, Lang, Welles or – heaven help us! – Stanley Kramer? Perhaps; but if so, one should then ask why *Song of Songs* – arguably superior as a Dietrich film to any of those by the directors listed above – is less well known than a title by George Marshall (*Destry Rides Again*), let alone one by Richard Boleslawski (*The Garden of Allah*). It doesn't make sense.

But then so many Mamoulian films haven't received the recognition they deserve. *City Streets* hasn't a high profile in the Gary Cooper filmography, let alone as a seminal gangster film. *Dr Jekyll and Mr Hyde*, while acknowledged by some as a masterpiece, isn't even recognised by most horror aficionados as a landmark of the genre; among fans of the musical, the same is probably true of *Love Me Tonight* and *Silk Stockings. Queen Christina* is probably better known for the anecdote about Garbo's *tabula rasa* playing in the final shot than for the film itself. *Becky Sharp* is more regularly cited – if it's cited at all – simply as the first Technicolor feature rather than as one of the most elegant and eloquently expressive of all colour movies. And many of the subsequent films, in terms of cinema history and criticism, have simply 'fallen off the radar', whereas by rights they should be celebrated, at the very least, as supremely stylish and enjoyable entertainment – or, more accurately, as prime examples of Golden-Age Hollywood film-making at its most artistically ambitious, adult, erudite and intelligent. So what happened?

Marlene Dietrich and Rouben Mamoulian on the set of *Song of Songs*

Tom Milne was clearly perplexed and disappointed by the critical neglect into which Mamoulian's once admirable reputation had already slipped by the late 1960s. But then Tom was a rather special critic who frequently managed to notice and understand a great deal more about a film than most of his colleagues. Some have argued, not without some justification, that he was the finest film critic Britain ever produced; whatever the merits of such an absolutist claim,[2] he was undeniably one of the country's most important and influential writers on film, contributing extremely valuable work on an amazingly wide range of movies and helping to change the way many British cinephiles thought about the cinema. Even the handful of monographs he wrote and edited – on Godard, Dreyer and Losey, in addition to the one on Mamoulian – testifies to an unusually catholic, open-minded approach. But then one should also recall his encyclopaedic knowledge of crime and horror films and musicals, and his often pioneering essays on Ozu, Rohmer, Franju, Melville, Sjøstrøm, Whale *et al.* Tom loved the cinema in all its variety, and his passion reveals the deep flaws inherent in the aforementioned old saw about critics being failed film-makers. He didn't want to make his own films, but he very much enjoyed passing on his enthusiasm to others – which is why, like most of the best critics, he concentrated primarily on writing about films and film-makers he admired rather than about those that aroused little enthusiasm in him. And his passion for all kinds of cinema ensured that he had little time for those false assumptions that arise from any simplistic distinctions made between high art and populist entertainment.

As anyone who reads what follows this foreword will discover, Tom's strengths as a critic were many. His writing was elegant, witty, and highly articulate. He was unusually adept at capturing, on the printed page, the tone, mood and import of a cinematic moment or sequence; he had a rare talent for identifying, isolating and describing those details of performance, dialogue, composition, movement, music, choreography, design or pacing that matter most. He was also an impressively astute analyst, alert to narrative structure, theme, motif, metaphor and all manner of resonance. More than most British critics of his generation, he understood that a movie was not just filmed literature or drama, and that it was therefore crucial to pay attention to its formal elements: a scene's rhythm might be as crucially significant at its narrative content. And far more than most British critics of the generations that followed his own, he knew that a movie doesn't exist in a vacuum; hence his many allusions not only to other films but to novels, poems, plays, paintings, songs and so on. It helped both that Tom was a voracious reader and that he had already, even before turning his attention, professionally, to cinema, edited a magazine of drama criticism. And it was most probably this fascination with the arts in general that made him particularly well attuned to the likewise erudite, formally syncretic approach to film-making favoured by Rouben Mamoulian.

By his own admission, Tom's purpose in writing his book on Mamoulian was 'dissent'. The director's work had given him so much pleasure that he wanted others to discover the films, so that they too might appreciate the consummate artistry of a widely forgotten talent. For that to happen, he felt that he had to challenge a couple of assumptions about Mamoulian held by those who'd written about his work. First, there was the widespread dismissive notion that it was 'all downhill' for Mamoulian after *Becky Sharp*; for Tom, who adored Mamoulian's two Fox films (*The Mark of Zorro*; *Blood and Sand*) and his three musicals (*High, Wide and Handsome*; *Summer Holiday*; *Silk Stockings*), such a charge was incomprehensible other than as the consequence of lazy thinking, a reluctance to approach the films on their own terms. Though Tom was right (as so often), we should perhaps bear in mind that very few critics were as well equipped as he to deal with some of these movies as thoroughly as he himself did. One wonders, for example, how many of those reviewers who had little time for *Summer Holiday* were familiar with O'Neill's *Ah, Wilderness!*, let alone with Swinburne, Omar Khayyám and Carlyle. The same probably goes for the response to Mamoulian's referencing of Spanish painters in *Blood and Sand* – whereas it's clear Tom not only knew the work of Velázquez, Goya, Murillo, El Greco *et al.* but understood precisely how and why Mamoulian used their respective styles to enhance the atmosphere and emotional dynamics of his film.

The second misapprehension that Tom set out to counter was the long-held, widespread belief that Mamoulian, if he was of any importance whatsoever, mattered more for a few specific innovations in film technique during the early years of sound cinema than for any more substantial achievement in creating a corpus of coherent, completed films. Read the following monograph and you'll see, once again, that Tom was right. He very effectively conveys how expressive and imaginative was Mamoulian's direction in deploying every tool at his command to create an uncommonly kinetic, meticulously choreographed style of filmic storytelling. (A cat-lover, Tom wrote with conspicuous delight: 'No wonder the Mamoulian trade-mark, making its appearance somewhere or other in each of his films, is that most graceful of creatures, the cat.') Watching a Mamoulian film, not only is one frequently exhilarated by the apparent effortlessness of the physical actions and gestures shown on screen; one is also caught up and carried along by the pace and rhythms of the storytelling itself, with music, dialogue and other sounds, not to mention superbly elastic editing, contributing to an impression of inexorable dramatic flow.

Here, however, we come to an intriguing question. If we are persuaded (as I am), either by Mamoulian's films or by Tom's advocacy thereof, that the former was indeed a major director, are we to understand that his particular artistry was akin to that of an orchestra conductor, interpreting the creations of others by imposing his own tonal, textural and rhythmic signature (or 'vision') through the skilful deployment of the various players and instruments at his disposal? If that is the case – and it's undoubtedly an integral part of what any proficient film director does – then we must certainly acknowledge Mamoulian as an unusually capable *'metteur en scène'*. But might we go still further? For even Tom didn't ask – and perhaps he simply didn't consider the question sufficiently significant – whether Mamoulian might perhaps also be seen as an 'auteur': as an artist with particular preoccupations of his own, rather than as a mere interpreter of someone else's ideas.

To some such a question might now seem quaintly old-fashioned, an echo of the auteurist arguments of the late 1950s, 60s and early 70s, but that doesn't necessarily mean that it isn't worth asking; after all, not being embraced as an artist who had something to say for himself, rather than as an adept interpreter of other people's material, may have been one of the factors that led to Mamoulian's undeservedly low standing among film critics and historians. And while I certainly wouldn't argue that Mamoulian was a fully-fledged auteur in the sense that one would apply that term to a Hitchcock or Hawks, a Ford or Fuller – let alone to a Fassbinder or Fellini, a Bergman or Bresson – I do think a case can be made for the idea that Mamoulian was attracted to a particular kind of story featuring a particular kind of character or characters. For he does appear to have returned repeatedly – albeit unintentionally, I'm sure, and probably unconsciously – to the related themes of duality and a 'divided' or conflicted personality.

Any such fascination on the director's part is most immediately evident, of course, in *Dr Jekyll and Mr Hyde*, where it not only serves as the subject of the film but also informs a great deal of Mamoulian's *mise en scène*. The oppositional split between the conjoined Jekyll and Hyde (who are, lest we forget, merely different sides of the same coin) is made manifest through Mamoulian's use of 'subjective' point-of-view shots and reflections in mirrors; through the doublings of Muriel and Ivy and of Muriel's father and Dr Lanyon; through the several allusions to angels and devils; through decor (most notably, hanging on the wall of Ivy's boudoir, the Velázquez painting known as 'the Rokeby Venus', in which, fittingly, the reclining nude gazes at her own face – otherwise invisible to us, since we see her from behind – in a mirror); and through the use of split screens, lengthy dissolves and sound overlapping from one scene to another.

Such thematic and formal motifs abound throughout Mamoulian's oeuvre. Even in his first feature, *Applause*, the dual focus is on a singer, torn between maternal and sexual love, and her daughter, torn between filial duty and romantic desire; Mamoulian enhances and embellishes this theme by highlighting and exploring contrasts between city and country, men and women, age and youth, 'reality' and appearance/performance, again making expressive use of split-screen editing, reflections and shadows, and overlapping sound. Thereafter, most of his protagonists (and quite a few antagonists, as it happens) are 'divided' in one way or another. In *Jekyll and Hyde*, the conflict is deadly in its effect on others as well as on the protagonist. Elsewhere, it is painful or damaging primarily in its effect on the divided character: it's a source of confusion, indecision, or of ill-advised ambition that results in loneliness or unhappiness. One thinks of Nan and the Kid in *City Streets*, the Princess in *Love Me Tonight*, Lily in *Song of Songs*, Christina in *Queen Christina*, Katusha and Dmitri in *We Live Again*, Joe and Lorna in *Golden Boy*, Juan in *Blood and Sand*, Ninotchka in *Silk Stockings*.

In other films, however, the duality is at least in part voluntary or even intentional, the product of a strategic performance embarked upon in order to attain some kind of ulterior objective; that is certainly true of Maurice in *Love Me Tonight*, Becky in *Becky Sharp*, Diego in *The Mark of Zorro*, even Susan and her 'con-mentors' in *Rings on Her Fingers*. But it's also important, here, to note that the division doesn't exist only within characters; the conflict is also external, in that there is almost invariably a gulf between the needs of the individual and the requirements or expectations of society. Indeed, whether the inner conflict is involuntary (as in the majority of cases) or strategic, it almost invariably arises *in response to* the various constraints placed upon the individual by the society in which he or she lives. Hence Jekyll rebels against the sexually repressive mores of 'respectable' Victorian society, Maurice the tailor questions how far class differences should dominate relationships between men and women, Christina finds political customs and monarchic traditions excessively restrictive of her freedom, Zorro conceals his true self beneath a foppish façade in order to fight tyrannical injustice, and Ninotchka discovers that her political ideology is at odds with certain more basic needs.

Time and again, then, we bear witness to some kind of clash between, on the one hand, an individual's desire and need for basic human freedoms and, on the other, society's restrictive notions of what is acceptable or permissible. And that conflict, in Mamoulian's films, is most often explored within the realm of pleasure and sexuality. In *Applause* we have the tawdry burlesque circuit and the predatory, pimp-like manager; in *Dr Jekyll and Mr Hyde* Jekyll's 'almost indecent' libertarian ideals and Ivy's nakedly seductive appeal; in *Love Me Tonight* a sleeping beauty who's not wasting away but 'just wasted'; in both *Queen Christina* and *The Mark of Zorro* upfront sexual ambiguity; in *Blood and Sand* a vampiric, bullfighter-collecting Doña Sol who represents 'death in the evening'. So it goes, all the way up to *Silk Stockings*' Ninotchka, who, after being told by her American suitor that he'd like to 'make a tour of you/, the arms, the eyes, the mouth of you/, the East, West, North and South of you', 'liberates' herself by dancing as she changes from strictly functional underclothes into more alluringly delicate Parisian lingerie.

Applause: Jack Cameron and Helen Morgan

It's intriguing, incidentally, that that final film's 'Satin and Silk' number, performed by Janis Paige in an altogether brassier hymn to feminine frillies, is verbally anticipated by Diego in *The Mask of Zorro* when, in discussion in his effete guise with Lolita's foolish mother, he professes a fascination with satins and silks. For all the customary elegance of Mamoulian's *mise en scène*, one should never underestimate his penchant for sly innuendo. Watch closely, for example, Astaire's glances and gestures as he performs the aformentioned lines from 'All of You'. Observe, too, in *Love Me Tonight*, the Count de Savignac expressing his regret at being unable to entertain the Princess as he'd hoped because he 'fell flat on his flute'; or Maurice already warning her, at their first encounter, that he'd 'like to have a little son of Mimi by and by'. *Song of Songs*, meanwhile, is quite extraordinary for the explicitness and abundance of its visual and verbal metaphors for sexual desire and activity. So is it really just accidental that the prelude – or foreplay – to the fateful seduction of Katusha in *We Live Again* occurs during the kissing rites at Easter Mass, with Dmitri repeatedly responding to the 'Christ is risen' call with a very evidently exhilarated 'He is indeed!'? It's tempting to dismiss the innuendo as fortuitous and unwitting – though we should perhaps also remember the interest with which Lolita notices a sword sticking out from beneath the folds of disguised Diego's monk's habit during a likewise highly charged church encounter in *The Mask of Zorro*. Such moments are, at any rate, sufficiently suggestive and numerous in Mamoulian's work for it to feel as if he may in fact have known exactly what he was doing.

The very fact that we cannot always be entirely sure as to Mamoulian's precise intentions in filming these and other similar scenes is yet further evidence, I feel, of the delicacy of touch that may be found everywhere in his work. Any such lightness, however, in no way precludes the existence of some sort of thematic consistency in his work. If indeed he did repeatedly make films dealing with characters who are somehow in crisis because their most basic requirements and impulses – the need, for example, for happiness and the freedom simply to be oneself – are threatened or oppressed by the constraining demands of the world they live in, that is perhaps not so very surprising.

For Mamoulian usually sided with his protagonists – and not only, one suspects, because Hollywood has always tended to prioritise the needs of the one over the many. There is a generosity extended to many of Mamoulian's characters that strikes one as unsentimental yet unusually 'unconditional', so that even the most foolish and weak and the most self-serving and arrogant among them – Kitty Darling, Jekyll, Becky Sharp and Juan Gallardo included – are recognised and respected as complex, often self-contradictory beings who are merely responding to the restrictive pressures exerted by society at large. The pursuit of simple, straightforward, individual happiness (and perhaps most especially of sexual or romantic fulfilment) seems to have been regarded by Mamoulian as wholly justifiable; and given that the director himself was something of a sensualist in terms of his concept of cinema, using all the syntactic tools at his disposal to bring pleasure to audiences, that is perhaps only appropriate. Tom notes Mamoulian's expertise in always constructing clear and succinctly evocative opening sequences, his skill in luring audiences into the carefully created worlds of his films; the aesthetic, with its accent on rhythm, harmony and elegance, was remarkably seductive. Not every Mamoulian film was a masterwork, but all of them are attractive and entertaining, and many unusually fine: subtle, sophisticated and lovely enough to warrant and reward repeated viewings. Tom's book shares those characteristics with the films that are its subject, and serves as a superb introduction to a neglected but important cinematic artist. Hopefully, his 'small tribute' to a film-maker who had given him great pleasure will help others to find much of value in an extraordinarily rich body of work – one that reminds me of some words spoken by Garbo's Christina: 'One could go out and get lost in it, and forget the world.'

Notes

1. 'Let us now praise famous men' – a phrase from the Book of Ecclesiasticus – was also the title of a book on which critic and author James Agee collaborated with photographer Walker Evans.

2. Clearly the likes of Robin Wood, Ray Durgnat and David Thomson would also be strong contenders for such a superlative, but I myself would certainly argue that Tom was at the very least their equal.

On set: the circus in *High, Wide and Handsome* (above) and the wedding in *Song of Songs* (below)

Introduction

Hollywood has always been notoriously cavalier about its creators: not merely the truculent, self-willed giants – the von Stroheims and the Orsons Welles – who were too big for its boots, but even the more modest men who played the box-office game but still contrived to turn out original, honest and remarkably personal films. Its history is littered with cast-offs, its legends peopled with the once famous, dreaming, like Norma Desmond, of a comeback. You're as good, they say, as your last picture; but what this means is that you're as employable as your balance sheet, comprising reputation, box-office returns and insurance risk, will allow.

In the mid-1930s, Rouben Mamoulian was a gilt-edged proposition, snatched from Paramount by MGM and entrusted not only with the direction of Garbo in *Queen Christina*, but with the first film in the new three-colour Technicolor process, *Becky Sharp*. From there on the story is one of decline. Not, virtually every historian of the cinema to the contrary, in Mamoulian, but in critical appreciation of his work, and more importantly, in his employment by the Hollywood studios.

Mamoulian himself tells a story, which may perhaps be told with equal veracity from a different point of view, but which does illustrate a terrible truth about the movie business. In 1944 he was assigned to direct *Laura* with Otto Preminger as producer, and early in the shooting disagreements cropped up between producer and director. Since Preminger at the time was a comparative newcomer to Hollywood, the studio offered to fire him; Mamoulian, knowing that he (Mamoulian) already had a reputation for being difficult, preferred to bow out gracefully since he was not particularly involved in the film anyway.

The moral is borne home by subsequent developments. In 1958 Mamoulian was set to direct the film version of his great stage success, *Porgy and Bess* (which had also been his first real success anywhere in its original, non-musical version of 1927). Pre-production disagreements had already sprung up with Samuel Goldwyn when a studio fire demolished the elaborate sets; by the time the production got under way again a couple of months later, Mamoulian had been fired and a new director – Preminger, as it happens – was in charge. Then, in 1961, came the great *Cleopatra* fiasco, and Mamoulian again bowed out after shooting some ten minutes of film. Angels don't like unfinished symphonies and Mamoulian's most recent film remains *Silk Stockings*, made in 1957. Meanwhile Mamoulian waits on the sidelines, along with King Vidor and all the other veterans who have been put out to pasture because they are too self-willed, because they are too old, because their health makes them bad insurance risks, because their last films didn't make enough money, or maybe just because.

Tragic enough at the best of times, this waste of talent is doubly so now at a moment when, for the first time in the history of the cinema, we are beginning to experience the rare pleasure of seeing films made by men who have grown up with the cinema, who have spent their lives making films, who are so immersed in technique that they transcend it. Serene, untrammelled masterpieces like *Le Caporal épinglé* (made by Renoir when he was sixty-seven), *Gertrud* (Dreyer at seventy-five), *Seven Women* (Ford at seventy-one) or *Belle de Jour* (Buñuel at sixty-seven). Young Citizen Kane, experimenting delightedly with his box of tricks, could not have made any of these films, any more than the young Henry James could have written *The Golden Bowl*; the Orson Welles of *Chimes at Midnight* and *The Immortal Story*, on the other hand, might yet. And any art, after all, needs the daring of old age as well as the very different daring of youth.

Parallel to this neglect by the studios, critical evaluation of Mamoulian's work seems to have solidified to a remarkable degree. Open almost any history of the cinema or volume of criticism and the story is the same: high praise of the early films, total neglect of the later ones. Almost invariably, Mamoulian is valued chiefly as an innovator: as the man who broke the sound barrier to liberate both camera and soundtrack in *Applause* (1929); who experimented with subjective sound (*City Streets*, 1931), subjective camera (*Dr Jekyll and Mr Hyde*, 1931), non-realistic sound (*Love Me Tonight*, 1932); and who paved the way for dramatic use of colour (*Becky Sharp*, 1935). Otherwise the Mamoulian history can be summed up, not unfairly, in two quotes: 'Mamoulian's tragedy is that of the innovator who runs out of innovations' (Andrew Sarris, *The American Cinema*); 'Since 1936, Mamoulian has made fewer and fewer films. Such productions as *High*, *Wide and Handsome* and *Blood and Sand* hardly displayed any recognisable personal touch' (Rotha and Griffith, *The Film Till Now*). Everything from *The Gay Desperado* to *Silk Stockings* is thus cheerfully consigned to oblivion.

So deeply ingrained is this attitude that even enthusiasts sacrifice to it. Giulio Cesare Castello, who wrote the first (and only) serious study of Mamoulian's work as a whole, does at least rescue *Summer Holiday*, but otherwise adheres to the traditional view that a steady decline began after *Becky Sharp* in 1935. Arthur Knight includes some of the most sympathetic and perceptive pages written about Mamoulian in his *The Liveliest Art*, but neglects to cite any film made after 1936, even though the book was published in 1957. Even Mamoulian himself seems to subscribe to the view that his films are important mainly because of their innovations and experiments. In interviews and in his comments made during personal appearances for a retrospective devoted to his work at the National Film Theatre in April 1968, he returns constantly to the same topics: the two separate sound channels mixed on a single track in *Applause*, the superimposition of Gary Cooper's voice over Sylvia Sidney's face in *City Streets*, the thunderous explosion accompanying the shattering of a vase in *Love Me Tonight*, the gradual suffusion of red over the screen during the Waterloo sequence in *Becky Sharp*. These technical advances, like the dramatic highlights which also recur in Mamoulian's reminiscences – the bedroom-stroking scene in *Queen Christina*, the transformations in *Dr Jekyll and Mr Hyde* – are undoubtedly important; but not to the exclusion of the films themselves, considered as a coherent, developing whole.

(*next page*) *Summer Holiday*: filming the dance after 'Afraid to Fall in Love'

The purpose of this monograph is therefore dissent. And I take as my basic text a quotation from Mamoulian when he was describing the famous 'symphony of noises' which illustrated the awakening of Catfish Row in his 1927 production of *Porgy*, and which he later incorporated into *Love Me Tonight*: 'In direction and staging, I used my favourite principle of integrating all theatrical elements into one stylised rhythmic pattern.'

Born in Tbilisi, Georgia, in 1898, Mamoulian came to the West as a disciple, more or less, of Stanislavsky. Back in Russia, while studying criminal law at Moscow University, he had joined the Second Studio at the Moscow Art Theatre, working under Vakhtangov; and when he landed his first professional assignment as a stage producer, the keynote of his work was relentless realism. The play was Austin Page's *The Beating on the Door*, and its first performance was at the St James's Theatre, London, in November 1922. The result from Mamoulian's point of view, as he later commented, was that 'This was the first and last production that I directed in this manner. I discovered I had no affinity for naturalism on the stage. In my subsequent work, my aim always was rhythm and poetic stylisation.' Turning down an offer from Jacques Hébertot in Paris, he went to America to help organise and direct the American Opera Company in George Eastman's brand-new theatre in Rochester, New York.

For the next two and a half years Mamoulian produced operas and operettas, ranging from *Tannhäuser* and *Pelléas and Mélisande* to *The Merry Widow* and *H.M.S. Pinafore* by way of *Rigoletto* and *Carmen*. 'Eastman, of course, was only interested in the musical aspects. I was already seeking a truly dramatic theatre, a theatre that would combine all the elements of movement, dancing, acting, music, singing, decor, lighting, colour and so on.'

Then came an offer from the Theatre Guild in New York. He produced three plays for the Theatre Guild School, one more in London, and in 1927 went back to the Guild for *Porgy*, a huge success, and the 'Symphony of Noises': 'The curtain rose on Catfish Row in the early morning. All silent. Then you hear the Boum! of a street gang repairing the road. That is the first beat; then beat 2 is silent; beat 3 is a snore – zzz! – from a Negro who's asleep; beat 4 silent again. Then a woman starts sweeping the steps – whish! – and she takes up beats 2 and 4, so you have:

Boum! – Whish! – zzz! – Whish!

and so on. A knife sharpener, a shoemaker, a woman beating rugs and so on, all join in. Then the rhythm changes: 4:4 to 2:4; then to 6:8; and syncopated and Charleston rhythms. It all had to be conducted like an orchestra.'

Anyone who has seen the electrifying opening sequence of *Love Me Tonight*, where this symphony is reproduced intact, will know that Mamoulian was by now ready to take to cinema like a duck to water – as in fact he did two years later with *Applause*, bringing to it an impeccable control of that essential element of moving pictures: movement. No wonder the Mamoulian trademark, making its appearance somewhere or other in each of his films, is that most graceful of all creatures, the cat. Movement to Mamoulian is like a brushstroke to a painter: the delicate, infinitely variable factor which can bring life to a still life, beauty to a human face, emotion to a landscape, transforming dross into gold. A rose is a rose until Renoir paints it. *The Mark of Zorro* is just another historical romance until Mamoulian films it.

Inside his brain there must be an invisible metronome almost as tangible as the one he used to control Garbo's exquisitely modulated movements in the sequence in *Queen Christina* where she wanders round the bedroom in the inn, touching, caressing, remembering the place where she found love. So much so that one is almost tempted to say that every Mamoulian film is a musical. It isn't true, of course, but with every action and every line of dialogue conceived in terms of stylised rhythm – *choreographed* rather than directed – it feels as though it were. *The Mark of Zorro*, for instance, opens with an effortless sequence, no more than a dozen brief shots, in which two rows of cadets going through their paces on horseback at the military academy in Madrid suddenly become, just for a moment, dancers in an elegant quadrille. *We Live Again*, his adaptation of Tolstoy's *Resurrection*, begins with a series of low-angled dissolves of fields and cows and horses, sensuously framed by trees heavy with blossom in a brilliant pastiche of Dovzhenko, until suddenly, appearing in unison over the skyline with the same burst of exhilaration as the three sailors in *On the Town*, come three horses and three ploughs. Even in *Dr Jekyll and Mr Hyde*, as Jekyll sits absorbed in playing the organ at the beginning of the film and is interrupted by his butler entering to remind him of his lecture, the dreamy repetition of the butler's name ('What is it, Poole? ... So it is, Poole, so it is. ... You know, Poole, you're a nuisance. ... All right, Poole, all right') makes a perfectly ordinary conversation echo like the introduction to a Rodgers and Hart song.

Witty, elegant, supremely stylish in the best sense of the word, Mamoulian films have as their real distinguishing mark their unerring sense of rhythm in exploring the sensuous pleasures of movement. Long before *On the Town* was hailed as a breakthrough for the way in which its musical numbers sprang naturally out of the action, Mamoulian was doing the same thing with such ease that it is often difficult to separate one from the other. (Equally difficult, often, to credit that action sequences like Zorro's escape from the chapel in *The Mark of Zorro*, or young Juan's flight from the tavern to the moonlit bullring in *Blood and Sand*, are not actually dance routines.) Even as early as 1932, with *Love Me Tonight*, Mamoulian's camera was so adept at simulating dance and musical rhythms round the characters that when they do break into song and dance, there is virtually no perceptible transition. By 1957 and *Silk Stockings*, his inimitable method of conjuring action, dialogue, songs and dances out of one magical, all-purpose hat, and expressing plot, emotion and meaning as freely by one as by the other, was one of consummate mastery. The film, incredibly, was written off by almost everybody as an aberration unworthy of its origins in the Lubitsch-Garbo *Ninotchka*.

What follows in this book may not convert anyone to Mamoulian; it may not even succeed in conveying what I feel about these films; but at least it will stand as a small tribute to a film-maker who has given me great pleasure.

1: *Applause*

1929 was the year of the great Coming of Sound panic in the film industry. Experienced stage producers were hurriedly summoned to cope with the problem, either as directors if they were famous enough, or as dialogue directors if they were not, and Mamoulian was lured away from Broadway – though not as far as Hollywood – by an offer from Jesse Lasky and Walter Wanger of Paramount. For five weeks he watched and absorbed the mechanics of film-making at the Astoria Studios in New York, where Herbert Brenon was at work and Jean de Limur was directing Jeanne Eagels in *Jealousy*. Then, at the same studios, having 'learned what not to do', he plunged straight into *Applause*, the story of an ageing burlesque queen who sacrifices herself for her daughter, set in the sleazy atmosphere of second-rate vaudeville halls, and edged from melodrama into tragedy by Helen Morgan's superb performance and by Mamoulian's cunning juggling of naturalism and expressionism into a stylised reality.

Remarkable enough even today, the film must have seemed – and indeed was hailed as – a real eye-opener in those days of talk, talk and more talk, stage-bound by cumbersome equipment enclosed in soundproof booths. The very opening sequence indicates that Mamoulian was thinking in terms of movement rather than sound, and in terms of cinema rather than theatre. It also, incidentally, establishes the elliptically swift, scene-setting opening which was to become almost a Mamoulian trademark.

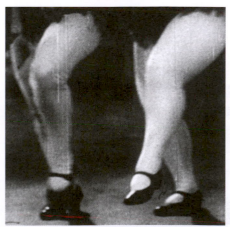

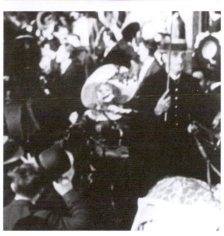

Applause: the opening sequence

A close-up of a shuttered store-front, the sign reading 'Zenith Feed Grain Supply Co.' The camera tracks back, cuts to a forlornly empty street with newspapers blown about by the wind, among them a theatre poster advertising 'KITTY DARLING, QUEEN OF HEARTS'. A small dog running on to worry the poster is rescued by a little girl just as the sound of a brass band swells up on the soundtrack, and we cut to Kitty Darling herself (Helen Morgan), making her triumphal progress through the crowded streets in an open carriage. The music changes to ragtime, the camera cuts inside a burlesque theatre, and tracks steadily left past the musicians in the orchestra pit; pans up, and tracks right along a row of fat, lackadaisically kicking legs; pans up yet further, and returns along the raddled faces of the row of weary, bumping and grinding chorus girls.

Apart from its sheer brilliance as film-making, the sequence is cleverly contrived as a foundation for the whole film. It plants the idea that Kitty's fame will be shortlived, undercutting the slightly hackneyed 'fickleness of fortune' theme by getting in first, as it were; and, more importantly, it establishes in terms of harsh, grimy lasciviousness the weary reality that lies behind that fame. Without it, what follows would soon have foundered in a sticky mess of sentiment as just another of those tearful mother-and-daughter epics that Hollywood is so fond of.

Kitty Darling, evidently pregnant, passes out while on stage with her clown partner and is carried to her dressing room. It transpires that she has received a telegram to say that her husband, under sentence of death, has been refused a pardon. The show goes on, and within minutes the news is brought on stage that Kitty has given birth to a daughter. Far from being risible, however, the sequence is remarkably effective, thanks to Mamoulian's stylised handling of it as an extension of the vaudeville turns we have been watching, with the clown appealing for a doctor in a cross-talk act with the audience ('Is there a doctor in the house?' – laughter – 'No foolin' boys, is there a doctor in the house?'), and the news of the birth brought on stage by one of the girls and passed from mouth to mouth to the clown, who yelps 'Oh! boy' and turns a delighted cartwheel offstage to Kitty's dressing room. There, following a superb close-up of Kitty's face, streaked with make-up and haloed in golden hair, comes the first clumsy touch of expressionism: as the chorus girls file past

the couch on which Kitty is lying to offer their congratulations, a shot vertically upwards shows a ring of faces peering down, and another vertically downwards shows the same ring round the couch – more Busby Berkeley than Mamoulian.

Thereafter, with the exception of another of these unconvincingly mannered and unmotivated overhead shots (which he never resorted to again), Mamoulian gets a grip on his expressionism, and brings it more and more into play as a counterpoint to the sordid reality of the burlesque theatre and the gracefully naturalistic iconography of the convent scenes. For Kitty – indeed, yes – sends her little girl to a convent school, whence she returns at the age of seventeen, knowing nothing of how her mother earns her living, to find Kitty ageing, slipping, and in the grip of an unscrupulous sponger who soon has his eye on pretty young April.

Applause: Helen Morgan as Kitty Darling

One only has to compare Mamoulian's handling of these convent scenes with that of almost any other Hollywood director – for instance, James Whale, himself no mean stylist, in the similar scenes in *Show Boat* – to realise that he was a master at stating the unstateable by understatement. No pious sermonising, no heavenly choir, no sticky embarrassment: simply an impression of almost Bressonian calm and intensity. When Joe the clown suggests that the child should be sent to a convent so that 'she'll grow up a lady', Kitty hesitates in an agony of indecision. 'Maybe I will,' she says, and Mamoulian cuts to a close-up of hands, pulling back the camera to reveal a nun talking to the child in a garden shrine, then pulling further back to reveal another nun praying under the spreading branches of a tree in the foreground, and finally moving in again on this image of almost pastoral simplicity before cutting back to Kitty, sitting on the floor sorting out old letters and souvenirs as she softly croons 'What Wouldn't I Do for That Man?' to a photograph of her lover, Hitch Nelson. A diagonal wipe, splitting the screen in two, reveals Hitch in his room kissing a girl

Applause: arrival at the convent

in deshabille; the wipe completed, Hitch – a city slicker in spats, tight-striped suit and patent-leather hair – leaves his room, crosses the corridor, removes a hair from his lapel, and bursts in on Kitty: 'Hello, beautiful!'

Already Mamoulian is adept in not wasting time. Having just made the transition from birth to childhood in one cut, he now leaps to adolescence in another. For as Hitch enters, Kitty is reading a letter from her daughter, now aged seventeen. Hitch insists that she be brought back to help the family finances; and Kitty, played throughout as a foolish, fond woman who loves not wisely but too well, tearfully consents when he threatens to leave her: 'It's her or me.' The scene ends with the introduction of a major expressionist motif: as Hitch comforts Kitty, assuring her that she has made the right decision and that they will be 'one big, happy family', his shadow looms, large and threatening, on the wall.

We cut back to the convent: a beautiful chiaroscuro sequence as April bids farewell to the Mother Superior, with the camera tracking slowly down corridors where nuns glide past or kneel in prayer, and out to the gardens where children play on the lawn, nuns stroll by the lake and swans float gracefully on the water. Largely silent, except for an 'Ave Maria' sung on the soundtrack, the scene enshrines a sense of pure tranquillity, almost as incorporeal as the nuns who flit like black and white shadows through it. 'Between the idea/And the reality/Between the motion/And the act/Falls the shadow,' wrote T. S. Eliot ('The Hollow Men'). A sequence shot on location in Penn Station amid the honking traffic and bustling crowds gives April her first taste of raw reality; but the real shock is reserved for another brilliant shadow-play when she is taken backstage at the burlesque theatre to see her mother.

The sleazy atmosphere of the opening recurs, intensified with a new cruelty. As Kitty goes on stage for her number, the audience jeers 'They ought to pension off that old blonde' in a montage of sneering, raddled faces and blackened teeth. Kitty's face dissolves into April's, watching in horror; and as Kitty goes on stage again for the finale in a scanty costume and fantastic feathered headdress, after excitedly greeting her daughter, April is further assailed by huge, obscene images, performing bumps and grinds in silhouette against the backcloth. The final turn of the screw comes in a ridiculous, wonderful, touching scene between mother and daughter at their hotel. 'Everything is so different from what I thought it would be,' cries April. 'It ain't

what you do, it's what you are,' replies Kitty, and gently sings her daughter to sleep: a luminously beautiful scene – April's hand reaching under the pillow for her crucifix, Kitty tenderly stroking her hair, neon lights flickering on and off outside the window – until suddenly a huge shadow appears on the wall behind them, and one realises that Hitch has just come in.

It was this sequence – three days into shooting – which gave Mamoulian his first experience of the perennial technician's cry of 'It's impossible', and which led him to take his first important step towards breaking the sound barrier by insisting on filming the scene in one shot, with Helen Morgan's lullaby and Joan Peers's whispered prayer recorded simultaneously. In his own words: 'But, they said, we couldn't record the two things – the song and the prayer – on one mike and one channel. So I said to the sound man, "Why not use two mikes and two channels and combine the two tracks in printing?" Of course it's general practice now; but the sound man and George Folsey, the cameraman, said it was impossible. So I was mad. I threw down my megaphone

Applause: Kitty at the Burlesque theatre

(all directors still used megaphones in those days) and ran up to Mr Zukor's office … "Look!", I said, "Nobody does what I ask …" So Zukor came down and told them to do it my way; and by 5.30 we had two takes in the can. Next day I went to the studio very nervous. But as I went in, the big Irish doorman, who'd always ignored me before, raised his hat and bowed. It seemed they'd had a secret 7.30 viewing of the rushes in the studio, and were so pleased with the result that they'd sent it straight off to a Paramount Sales Conference. After this, what Mamoulian said, went.'

Mamoulian's chief motivation, of course, was to unchain the camera: 'In those days, a scene was shot with three cameras, two for close-ups, one for long shot. And then into the cutting room to intercut the three. I insisted on a fluid camera which would pan freely, as well as move in and out of a scene.' And although *Applause* relies more on expressionistic effects than the overall rhythmic flow which begins to appear in *City Streets* and is brought to the level of a fine art in *Love Me Tonight*, the camera does frequently move with characteristic wit, nowhere more so than in the inspection of the chorus line at the beginning, or in the slow lateral track which marks the beginning of April's idyll with a young sailor. After the show one night – April having become a reluctant showgirl – as Kitty goes off to a spare-time job hostessing at a stag party, Hitch waits with lecherous intent to take April home, while April slips quietly out into the street. At sidewalk level, the camera follows her feet through a maze of dustbins, pauses as she stops to attend to a bothersome shoe, and notes a pair of watching sailor feet, which turn and follow as a dog yaps in the background and a white kitten (first appearance of the Mamoulian mascot) crosses their path.

Also alone and lonesome, the sailor takes her to a cafeteria and romance blossoms. The dialogue is hackneyed, the kind of *faux-naif* folk idiom which Odets later made his speciality. Asked what his name is, the sailor answers, 'Tony. I don't like it much. Sounds like a wop bootblack.' Then, 'Gee, but your eyes are blue.' Yet it also rings tender and true because Mamoulian infuses their scenes together – falling in love in the seedy, deserted restaurant; dreaming together on Brooklyn Bridge as they watch the ships put out to sea; finding their first kiss under the open sky on the roof of a skyscraper as an aeroplane soars overhead – with a simple lyricism which is neither *faux* nor *naif*.

Kitty is delighted, Hitch furious, when April announces her decision to quit the stage to marry Tony. When April then overhears Hitch tell her mother that she is old, washed-up, and that April is her 'meal-ticket from now on', the stage is set for a grand climax of self-renunciation, which Mamoulian orchestrates brilliantly as Hitch storms out with a sneering 'See you in show business, beautiful', and Kitty, sinking down by the table to find herself staring at a photograph of herself as she once was, rises to gaze wonderingly at the ageing face reflected in the mirror. Tragedy is secure in Helen Morgan's superbly ravaged face at that moment, and the cross-cutting that follows, though a trifle dated now, still works. In the flat, Kitty suddenly smiles to herself and, tremulous with excitement, searches the bathroom cabinet for a bottle of poison; in the restaurant where they are supposed to be celebrating their engagement, April forces herself to tell Tony that she is giving him up to go back to the stage. Having unburdened herself, April asks for a glass of water, and as she lifts it to her lips, we dissolve to Kitty drinking the poison. Even here Mamoulian's rhythmic sense stands him in good stead. Instead of plunging head first into the finale, he pauses. Kitty, as though suspended in some vision

The last sequence of *Applause*: Joan Peers and Helen Morgan

of hell, sits at the window in a rocking chair, her face flickeringly illuminated and plunged into darkness by the neon lights, while the traffic honks and screeches below. Meanwhile, in one of those offhand little naturalistic touches which are so cunningly deployed throughout the film, April sees Tony off on the subway; neither can think of anything to say, and Tony almost absently puts a coin in a slot machine; as his train pulls in, he suddenly becomes aware of the sticks of chewing gum in his hand, and thrusts them at her like a love token as he runs for the train.

After this the ending, melodramatic or not, has the same direct, overwhelming attack as the last scenes of *Tol'able David* or *Stella Dallas*. The dying Kitty staggers to the theatre in search of her daughter. April, arriving to go back on the stage, finds her lying, presumed drunk, on the couch in her dressing room (same couch, same posture as in the scene of April's birth), and offers to take her place. She is a wild success, and as she retreats from the applause, Tony is there, waiting and now understanding. They embrace against a poster advertising Kitty Darling in 'Parisian Flirts', as the camera pans up to rest on Kitty's smiling face.

Applause has its faults, but they are mainly in the acting. Fuller Mellish, in particular, overplays grotesquely as the city slicker, while both he and Jack Cameron (as Kitty's clown friend) employ that flat, wisecracking delivery which is peculiarly of the 30s and which makes perfectly inoffensive lines, such as 'I got plans. I'm headin' for Broadway', sound absurdly overstated. Joan Peers, too, simpers overmuch, and is not exactly convincing in the leggily clumsy dance which supposedly brings out the roar of the crowd. Mamoulian obviously concentrated his attention on Helen Morgan, who is nothing short of superb. Already something of a legend as a torch singer in cabaret, this was her first film role, and she brings to it something of the wistful, ravaged quality that Judy Garland revealed in *A Star is Born*. It is a tragedy that with the possible exception of Whale's *Show Boat*, where she plays the role of the star-crossed Julie Laverne for everything it is worth – and, incidentally, gives a truly fabulous rendering of 'Bill' – the cinema was never again to find her a part worthy of her talent.

2: City Streets

After *Applause*, which was a critical rather than a box-office success, Mamoulian returned to Broadway, where he produced five plays and one opera – Schönberg's *The Hand of Fate* – before embarking on his second film, this time in Hollywood. Although *City Streets* tells a typical gangster tale of bootlegging, hijacking and mob rule, it is not, strictly speaking, a gangster film. For one thing, not a single killing is shown happening on screen; for another, Big Fella Maskal, the gang boss, has really more in common with George Bancroft's strutting, vainglorious Bull Weed in Sternberg's *Underworld* (made in 1927) than with the characters immortalised by Cagney, Edward G. Robinson, Paul Muni, *et al*. The conventions of the gangster films, with their defiant heroes taking on the whole world and spraying the streets with machine-gun bullets, were yet to be defined, on the basis of *Little Caesar* (1930), by *Public Enemy* (1931) and *Scarface* (1932). Instead, *City Streets* is first and foremost a love story, looking back to *Underworld* in its relationships and its stylised view of gangsterdom, and forward (though less doom-ladenly) to Lang's *You Only Live Once* in its story of young love at odds with society.

Again the opening is characteristic. A close-up of Sylvia Sidney's face as one eye mysteriously closes; the camera tracks back, and cuts to reveal the targets in a fairground shooting-stall as Nan (Sylvia Sidney) suddenly cries out, 'Hey, look out, what do you think you're doing?' and pushes aside a rifle waveringly aimed by a careless sharpshooter at The Kid (Gary Cooper) as he sets up the targets. The Kid promptly abandons his post to take Nan round the fair (STALL-OWNER, *CROSSLY*: 'You're fired. Where are you goin'?' – THE

City Streets: Gary Cooper and Sylvia Sidney

KID: 'Supper!' – STALL-OWNER: 'All right, but be back in half an hour'), flipping coins for hot dogs, winning toy elephants at sideshows, showing off a little as she fondly admires him. Having thus established their budding relationship with exemplary economy, Mamoulian then rocks the boat by a rare indulgence in the pathetic fallacy.

As the young couple stroll romantically along the moonlit beach, they talk. She tries to persuade him to think big and join the bootleggers she works for:

NAN: You sure pick jobs with no dough. Why don't you let me talk to Pop? He could put you in right.

THE KID: I wish you weren't in that racket. You'd have different ideas about things.

NAN: What have your ideas got you? … Racketeers are smart, not dumb like some people I know.

City Streets: the fairground

They quarrel: cut to waves dashing furiously on a rock. They make up and kiss: cut to waves rolling smoothly in. This is, however, the last real mistake in the film. As Nan and The Kid realise how late it is and start to run along the beach, Mamoulian dissolves to a birdcage for the first in a series of easy arabesques where the sensuous grace of the camera movement is compounded by the wealth of information conveyed without a word of explanatory dialogue. Moving slowly down from the birdcage, the camera pans slowly round a tawdry room, past an open drawer strewn with bullets, to an armchair where Pop Cooley (Guy Kibbee) sits reading the funnies, feet up and smoking a cigar, just as Nan enters. 'Where you bin?' he asks, twisting her arm. 'Out with that shooting-gallery mug again?'; then he grins, 'Good kid, you won't tell nobody nothin', and gives her some money as a reward. Then, as he goes out, he gently covers the cage: 'Jackie ain't sung all day. I'm worried about him.'

On one level, with the bird an obvious symbol for Nan, the scene is extremely simple, telling us all we need to know about the easygoing but ruthless Pop and his relationship with the girl. But it also, more subtly, serves as an oblique foreshadowing of the following sequence, its imagery – bird, bullets, Pop, girl not squealing, bird snuffed out – unmistakably telling the story of the murder which will now be planned and executed without a word being directly spoken.

As Pop Cooley leaves after covering the birdcage, a direct cut shows him getting out of a car, strolling down the corridor of an apartment block on his way to see one of the mob, Blackie, and pausing as he sees Big Fella Maskal (Paul Lukas) dallying with Blackie's girl outside the apartment. As the door opens and Blackie whisks the girl inside, yelling 'Stay away from my girl', Pop retreats prudently, then strolls casually forward to meet the Big Fella, who pauses. 'If anything happened to Blackie, do you think you could hold his mob together?' Then, 'I'd be willing to do business with you – if anything happened to Blackie.' As the Big Fella moves on, Pop lights a cigar pensively, looks at the match, snuffs it out and throws it away. Murder planned.

Murder executed. Pop enters the apartment, 'Hello, Blackie, how's tricks?' The girl is on the floor, evidently having just been beaten up. 'Use your phone?' asks Pop cheerfully, as the morose Blackie goes out. Beside the telephone, a sinuous statuette of a white cat. As Nan answers – beside her the toy elephant won at the fair – Pop tells her to meet him in half an hour, stressing '… *if you have to break your arm to get there*'. Then, jovially, to Blackie's girl, 'Anything wrong, sweetheart?' Beside her, a matching statuette of a black cat, and she swears revenge for her beating-up. A swift, predatory cut back and forth between the two cats as Pop's voice, off, smoothly continues, 'Suppose he don't live that long?' and back comes the reply, 'He'll get his some day.' Pop lights a cigar, casually remarks on how ash builds on the tip, carefully lays down the burning cigar on an ashtray, and goes out with a cheerful 'See you soon, Maggie.' Staring at the cigar, Maggie gingerly picks it up and takes a puff.

Cut to alarm bells, scurrying police, crowds gathering, Nan loitering alone, nervous, her arm in a sling. A cop stops her, and when she says she saw a girl running down the street, he turns. She goes off left, the cop right, and the camera stays put. After a moment, the cop reappears, looking after Nan. Cut again, to Pop being questioned in Blackie's apartment, coolly smoking his alibi – the cigar with its long, precarious tip of undisturbed ash.

The whole sequence is a brilliant, almost bravura display of pure cinema which leaves one in no doubt that Mamoulian knew and had thoroughly absorbed the techniques of the silent film. As always in his work at its best, dialogue is strictly an adjunct: important, but not *necessary* to an understanding of the action. Here, the words are almost like stress marks, indicating the accents in a verse where the poetry is carried by the images, the rhymes by the editing and camera movements. From beginning to end, in fact, from the bird-cage to the shot of Pop carefully balancing the cigar, the sequence is constructed – to use a rather fanciful comparison – like a sonnet, in which one main idea is fleshed out through a rigorous system of rhymes and remains incomplete until the last line. (Parenthetically: Mamoulian has sometimes been taken to task for overstatement in cross-cutting between the two cat statuettes. And it is undeniably true that, today at least, the mere presence of the statuettes would be enough to complete the symbolism of the sequence. But the mistake is an endearing one: since the Mamoulian mascot does not appear in live form elsewhere in the film, it seems only just that he should be allowed to animate them a little.)

After this there is a long, ragged patch in which individual sequences are effective but the overall rhythm is lost. Nan being questioned in the police

City Streets: Guy Kibbee and Sylvia Sidney at the police station, and the meeting at the prison

station, with the shadow of a barred door on the wall behind her as she is conned into taking the blame for the killing and goes to jail. The Kid demonstrating his prowess with a six-shooter at the fairground, and being persuaded to join the gang so that he will be able to earn the money to help Nan. Nan expressing her disillusionment to a fellow convict. And of course the celebrated sequence when The Kid, now resplendent in fur-collared coat and homburg hat, visits Nan in jail to tell her how he has taken her advice and joined the beer racket, and she is subsequently haunted in her cell by his voice. At the time, the slow track in to Nan's face as The Kid's voice echoes on the soundtrack, with the word 'Beer!' repeated and distorted in mockery, must have seemed a triumph of daring. Now, after umpteen imitations, it merely looks clumsy; and what one remembers from the scene is a tiny moment (also much imitated but never quite so true and tender) when they stand forlornly on either side of the iron grille. 'I wish . . . I wish I could just touch you,' says Nan. They lay their hands palm to palm, still separated by the thick mesh, and through it, only just, their lips brush in a kiss.

With Nan's release from jail, the narrative flow begins to pick up again, and the film abandons the sign of the caged bird for that of a great winged eagle as Nan and The Kid fight back to regain their liberty. First glimpsed as The Kid brings Nan back to the house he and Pop Cooley have moved into since their elevation in the organisation, the eagle – a bronze statue above a huge mirror in the hallway – is simply part of the decor, a hint of their new sybaritic existence, confirmed as Pop coyly calls 'Oh, Pansy!' up the stairs and a blonde floozie, guzzling chocolates at her dressing table in a frilly negligee, comes pattering plumply and poutingly down. Subsequently, totally unstressed but inescapably present, it assumes the temper of a double-edged symbol (revenge or retribution) when The Kid decides to force a showdown with Maskal (who wants Nan for himself). The Kid – as we have just seen from the way he disposes of two gunmen sent to kill him – is eagle-eyed enough to be able to take care of himself. But Nan, fearful of Maskal's vengeance, decides to bargain herself against The Kid's safety; and a remarkable shot, again unstressed but inescapable, shows her telephoning in the hall with the eagle casting its shadow over her.

This last third of the film, unfortunately, is marred initially by Paul Lukas's embarrassingly inadequate performance. In general, Mamoulian seems much happier here with actors than he was in *Applause*, especially his supporting cast (Kibbee, Wynne Gibson, Betty Sinclair), but Paul Lukas's suave, Middle European persona just does not mix with the tough jargon he is asked to deliver. When a mobster comments 'Hot stuff, eh chief?' at their first meeting with Nan, and Lukas answers with fervent but startling inappropriateness, 'Red hot!', one is forcibly reminded of the wisdom of Hermione Gingold's famous dictum, 'Don't take the words out of my mouth. You don't know *where* they've been.' Admittedly, familiarity has now bred a certain contempt for the gangster small-talk ('You're gettin' too big in this mob' or 'I'm runnin' this show'), but at least with the rest of the cast the effect is quaint rather than discomforting. Equally disastrous are Maskal's subsequent attempts to seduce Nan during a celebration dinner at a night club: the clash between the manner of Charles Boyer and the language of Humphrey Bogart is not a happy one.

Partly because of Lukas's performance and partly because the mood wavers, the nightclub sequence, which has the two men squaring up to each other on the dance floor amid the Chinese lanterns, never acquires the subtle textures of the similar scene at the gangsters' ball in *Underworld*. As Andrew Sarris comments (in *The Films of Josef von Sternberg*): 'Sternberg's hoodlums, like Cocteau's motorcyclists in *Orphée*, partake of the manners and machinery of the modern world without ever escaping from the dream world of their creator.' Much the same can be said of Mamoulian's characters, living out their dream of pure romance in an expressionist underworld; but in this particular sequence, for the only time in *City Streets* apart from the fairground crowd scenes (which have their own stylisation in any case), a clumsy, disrupting half reality keeps breaking through, especially when Maskal browbeats some innocent diners at the next table who are denizens of neither the modern nor the dream world.

With Nan's arrival at his apartment on her mission of self-sacrifice, however, Lukas comes briefly into his own as the suave seducer in silken dressing gown, soon to be shot by his discarded mistress, Agnes. The scene is handled as brilliantly and as elliptically as the murder of Blackie, and yet very differently. Given her marching orders a little earlier, Agnes is seen leaving as Nan arrives. Changing her mind, she steals out on to the balcony and sees Maskal relieve Nan of her handbag, take out her gun ('Now is that nice?'), and toss it casually away on a chair. The seduction continues, and as Maskal

telephones to keep his side of the bargain by reprieving The Kid, the door opens quietly behind them, a hand picks up the gun, removes the key from inside the door, and aims. Cut to McCoy, Maskal's lieutenant, with the phone in his hands as two shots echo dully over the wire. Then the hand drops the gun, the door is locked from the outside, and Agnes's voice is heard screaming for help. Where the earlier scene of Blackie's murder relied on a stylised pattern woven out of dialogue, gesture and symbolism, here the basis is purely rhythmic. Cutting unerringly on and with the movement within the frame, Mamoulian creates an extraordinarily vivid feeling that the camera has never once left the prime object of its interest, and has been circling round the couple in the room, watching the obscure workings of their fate, in one continuous, unbroken movement. It is perhaps the first fully realised example of a technique which Mamoulian was to develop almost into a principle.

City Streets: Accusation of murder. Wynne Gibson and Sylvia Sidney

After this, little remains except to bring about a happy ending, which is done with commendable dispatch. The Kid blusters his way into leadership of the mob; insists on driving the car taking Nan for a ride, along with three suspicious mobsters to see justice done; and drives so fast along precipitous mountain roads that the gunmen are only too glad to be allowed to get out while the lovers forge ahead to a new life. The last shot, completing the symbolic motif of the film, is of birds wheeling in the sky. Although *Applause* and *City Streets* are the only two Mamoulian films to be dominated by expressionism and/or symbolism, both recur from time to time, notably in *Song of Songs* and *Golden Boy*; and he never really lost his taste for lowering shadows and looming statuary, which are to him what fishnets and feathers were to Sternberg.

3: *Dr Jekyll and Mr Hyde*

For his third film, Mamoulian again tackled a popular genre, and his first and only venture into the world of horror remains by far the best of all the various adaptations of Stevenson's novella. One might perhaps argue that John Barrymore in 1920, or Jean-Louis Barrault in Renoir's *Testament du Docteur Cordelier*, had outdone Fredric March; but no one has come within miles of equalling the film's marvellous chiaroscuro vision of Stevenson's London as a fog-laden, gaslit warren of glistening streets, towering stairways and shabby dens, haunted by the shadow of Mr Hyde, alternately bestially small or towering like a giant, as he prowls with black cloak swirling like a matador's cape.

To anyone inured to Hollywood's long tradition of discreet evasion, the first thing that strikes one about Mamoulian's *Jekyll and Hyde* is its unequivocal sexual basis. Stevenson, of course, made no bones about the fact that Hyde indulged the unmentionable lusts that Jekyll only dreamed about, and the various adaptations have all seized on the point to explore Hyde's pleasures with varying degrees of gusto and frankness. But this version scripted by Samuel Hoffenstein and Percy Heath, slipping in under the Production Code net before the new powers of sanction made the going tougher in 1934, is alone in openly tracing the cause of Jekyll's troubles to the frustration by society of his own perfectly natural, unorgiastic desires.

At his very first meeting with his fiancée Muriel (Rose Hobart), Jekyll hints at his urgency: 'I can't wait any longer. We shall go to Devon for our honeymoon and live on love and strawberries and the sight of the sea ... Oh, I do love you seriously, so seriously that it – it frightens me. You've opened a gate

for me into another world. Before that my work was everything. I was drawn to the mysteries of science, to the unknown. But now the unknown wears your face, looks back at me with your eyes.' Jekyll's tone is light and almost bantering, but the point is neatly underlined when he urges his impatience on Muriel's father in the hope that they will be allowed to bring forward the date of the wedding: 'This is positively indecent,' snorts the General. Almost immediately, his healthily normal desires are wittily visualised – and sharply condemned – in the gently funny scene where he and Dr Lanyon, on their way home from the Carew mansion, encounter the sluttish Ivy Pearson (Miriam Hopkins) being beaten up in the streets. Escorting her home, Jekyll offers his services as a doctor. 'Look where he kicked me,' complains Ivy, provocatively drawing her skirts up to reveal a shapely leg. After an innocent flirtation ('By the way, you must not wear so tight a garter … It … er … impedes the circulation.'), Jekyll leaves, with Ivy's leg – in superimposition – teasing his mind with pleasant recollection, and Lanyon's voice destroying it:

LANYON: I thought your conduct quite disgusting, Jekyll.

JEKYLL: Conduct? Why, a pretty girl kissed me. Should I call the constable? Even suppose I'd liked it? …

LANYON: Perhaps you've forgotten you're engaged to Muriel?

Dr Jekyll and Mr Hyde: Stevenson's London

JEKYLL: Forgotten it? Can a man dying of thirst forget water? And do you know what
would happen to that thirst if it were denied water?

LANYON: If I understand you correctly, you sound almost indecent.

After this spirited defence of the sexual instinct, however, Jekyll reveals a curious moral confusion, illustrating Mamoulian's remark (interview with Jean Douchet and Bertrand Tavernier in *Positif*) that what interested him in Stevenson's story was not so much the conflict between Good and Evil, but between Nature and Civilisation. This subtle but important distinction is charted at the end of the conversation with Lanyon, when the latter, acknowledging the existence of man's baser instincts, urges the ostrich morality: 'We have to accept certain things.' Angrily, Jekyll retorts, 'I don't want to accept them. I want to be clean, not only in my conduct, but in my innermost thoughts and desires. And there's only one way to do it ... Separate the two natures in us.'

In other words, where Stevenson's Jekyll seeks his Hyde in order to indulge pleasures he recognises to be sinful, Mamoulian's Jekyll refuses to acknowledge that these pleasures are sinful, but is forced by society to behave as though he did. Interestingly, the creature he releases is an almost clinically exact copy of the psychotic killer – for instance, the Boston Strangler – whom psychiatry reveals more and more to be a product of social pressures, and whose nature seems to demand sadistic rather than sexual gratification. Jekyll's encounter with Ivy is suffused with a heady eroticism, carried over into the music-hall sequence in her singing of 'Champagne Ivy' and her lewd banter with the customers; but Hyde brings with him a cold chill which instantly snuffs out Ivy's warmth, and the gesture with which he whips the shawl from her naked shoulders as he talks of finding a place for her, 'A place to set off that fine body of yours', strips her to the bone with the pitiless efficiency of a piranha fish. Their relationship develops as a mounting orgasm of cruelty – first in the landlady's hints of brutality, then in Hyde's series of cat-and-mouse games with the terrified Ivy ('Well, if you don't hate me, you must love me. Isn't that so, my little one? Isn't it?'), until he finally traps her in a lie about her visit to Jekyll to ask for help, and strangles her: 'I'm going to take you in my arms now and hold you close ... close, my little lamb, my dove, my birdling ... There, my sweet. There, my dove. There, my little bride. Isn't Hyde a lover after your own heart?' Throughout, the equation for sex is never Ivy, always Muriel, as Jekyll makes repeated efforts to persuade Muriel to either marry him immediately or run away with him. And his final, despairing visit to her, when he realises he can no longer control his transformation, is tantamount to a bleak acknowledgement of his error, of all he hoped Hyde would find but did not: 'If I could take you in my arms; if I could only touch you! Oh, think of it. I daren't even touch you ever again in this world or the next.'

In an unexpected departure from his normal impressionistic practice, Mamoulian begins *Dr Jekyll and Mr Hyde* with the celebrated sequence seen from Jekyll's point of view, opening with a shot of organ pipes as a Bach fugue peals out, panning down to a close-up of hands on the keyboard, and remaining stubbornly subjective – sheet music on the organ, butler entering to remind him of his lecture, his reflection in the hall mirror as he puts on his hat and cloak, climbing into a carriage, arriving at the university – until he enters the lecture room, when the camera pans round in a 360° arc and, on the first word of his lecture, 'Gentlemen . . .' cuts to the back of the auditorium for the first objective view of Jekyll himself. Many interpretations and justifications have been offered for this sequence, all valid. Arthur Knight, for instance, notes that 'the subjective camera built a growing suspense, a curiosity about the appearance of the man we know will turn into the monstrous Hyde'. Mamoulian himself has said that he wanted to draw the audience into Jekyll's brain, to create an experience in which – as with the transformations – 'the audience does not see him – they *are* him'. But it is also, and perhaps most importantly, a subtle introduction to the Nature-Civilisation theme, with its unmistakable progression from moonstruck joyousness to strait-laced sobriety. At the outset, Jekyll's behaviour, the music, his inconsequential banter with Poole, are the paean of joy of a man in love; but from the moment he is glimpsed in the mirror, the celebrated Dr Jekyll arrayed for the public eye, the mood changes, constables and doormen bow obeisance, and the soundtrack rings with obsequious phrases, 'Good afternoon, Sir', 'Yes, Sir', 'How do you do, Sir'. In effect, what we are watching here is the first transformation scene: not of Jekyll into Hyde, but of Hyde – the man of passion – into Jekyll.

(next page) 'Come back soon, won't you . . . ?': Frederic March and Miriam Hopkins

Possibly unintentionally, Mamoulian gives another twist to the schizophrenic theme by using the diagonal wipe he first employed in *Applause* to introduce Muriel on her first appearance. Following the lecture, Lanyon and Jekyll visit the hospital, and despite Lanyon's protests that they will be late for their dinner engagement, Jekyll insists that he must operate at once on one of the free ward patients. He asks Lanyon to make his excuses to General Carew, adding that he will offer his own to Muriel later; and the diagonal wipe leaves Jekyll and his patient on one half of the screen, Muriel in her ball gown on the other, suggesting a further conflict between Jekyll's love and his desire to do (or be seen to do) good. Intentional or not, the device is not particularly important thematically, but it does illustrate the care with which Mamoulian *constructs* the rhythm of his films, taking into account not only dramatic impetus, but continuity of movement and continuity of emotion as well. Here, the diagonal wipe is completed to leave Muriel in command of the full screen; and when Lanyon arrives to deliver his message, a slow, caressing pan down her dress,

Dr Jekyll and Mr Hyde: Hyde arrives at the music hall; Hyde looks for Ivy

dissolving into a shot of her dancing at the ball, evokes the yearning desire Jekyll feels for her and which, when he does finally arrive, he articulates in the love scene in the garden bower.

The same device, for instance, subsequently links the two women, Ivy and Muriel, again evoking the schizophrenic theme, but this time also carrying the suggestion that Jekyll/Hyde is losing control of his ability to distinguish between his two selves and between the two women. With Muriel's return from the country, Jekyll has resolved never to release Hyde again, and it is the irreproachable, public-figure Jekyll who determines to compensate Ivy by sending her £50. Ivy receives the money as her landlady is dressing wounds inflicted on her back by Hyde, and a diagonal wipe brings Muriel into frame just as Jekyll arrives and successfully persuades the General to agree to their marriage. As the delighted Jekyll leaves, a dissolve takes him home for a rapturous – 'If music be the food of love, play on' – repetition of the opening scene at the organ, which conjures not Muriel, but Ivy, come to thank him for the money and to beg his help against Hyde. As Ivy leaves, with Jekyll's assurance that Hyde will never reappear, a direct cut takes us to Muriel awaiting his arrival for dinner, another to Jekyll striding on his way through the park. There a splendid visual metaphor resumes the four characters – Jekyll, Hyde, Ivy, Muriel – in one tight knot of terror. Jekyll sits enraptured on a park bench to listen to a nightingale, and as he starts to quote Keats, 'Thou wast not born for death, immortal Bird . . .', a black cat creeps stealthily through the branches and Jekyll begins, at first with horror and then with exultation, to turn into Hyde. Once again a diagonal wipe, from Muriel at the dinner party lamenting Jekyll's absence, to Ivy in her room as Hyde enters to strangle her.

As the terrified Ivy stumbles away from Hyde and falls behind the bed, where he crouches triumphantly over her, the murder takes place entirely out of sight, leaving the screen dominated by a statuette of two white, angelic figures embracing (in fact a copy of Canova's 'Cupid and Psyche'): an intimation, if any is still needed after the complex cross-currents sustained throughout the narrative of the entire sequence, that the purity of thought and desire sought by Jekyll is merely a chimera, ending figuratively in the death of Muriel, whom he can never see again, and actually in his own death. It is worth noting that just before her death, in toasting Jekyll for delivering her from Hyde, Ivy sees the

two men as angel and devil: 'Here's hoping that Hyde rots wherever he is, and burns where he ought to be. And here's hoping that Dr Jekyll will think of Ivy once in a while. He's an angel. Here's to you, my angel.' On the last line, Hyde enters; and the question implied by the film is, which is the angel, which the devil? Or, rather, can they be seen as separate entities?

In any adaptation of Stevenson's story, the transformation scene is inescapable: the audience is sitting waiting for the moment when handsome Jekyll will be metamorphosed into the deformed and diabolical Hyde, and Mamoulian plays the game brilliantly. To this day he has refused to reveal the secret of how the transformations were achieved in front of the camera, but it is not difficult to guess that they were done with coloured filters, changed to reveal different layers of make-up, and given a hallucinatory sense of actually happening before our eyes by the extraordinary soundtrack.[1] Our first glimpse

Dr Jekyll and Mr Hyde: the last farewell to Muriel. Rose Hobart and Frederic March

of the completed transformation as Hyde stares at himself in the mirror, panting 'Free! Free at last!' or holds his face exultantly up to the rain on his first venture out, is of a devil incarnate. But the real chill of horror in the film comes at the end, after Jekyll's visit of farewell to Muriel. Unable to bear the thought of never seeing her again, he stands staring at her in the darkness outside the french windows, and a shot of his hands reveals that he is changing into the familiar, dwarfish figure of Hyde. Instead, the dark, cloaked figure at the window swells in stature, proud and erect, not Hyde but a Luciferian Jekyll.

Structurally, thematically and psychologically, *Dr Jekyll and Mr Hyde* is masterly, and superbly executed in Karl Struss's velvety, glowing camerawork. Here and there the tone falters – in the slightly overwrought transformation scenes (more Stevenson's fault than Mamoulian's) or in the scene where Jekyll reveals his secret to Lanyon, with the latter towering over him like a judge behind his desk in a sudden reversion to the heady expressionism of the earlier films. Here and there, too, the acting falters, with Rose Hobart making a rather pallid Muriel (no challenge to Miriam Hopkins's splendid Ivy), and Fredric March, as so often in his films of the early 1930s, simpering unhappily through the romantic scenes (but coming into his own as Hyde). The blemishes are minor, but enough to leave the honour of being Mamoulian's first flawless masterpiece to *Love Me Tonight*.

4: *Love Me Tonight*

Blown in to Hollywood by the same sound storm that brought Mamoulian came the wittiest and perhaps the greatest song-writing team Broadway has ever known. Richard Rodgers and Lorenz Hart had made an inauspicious Hollywood début in 1931 by writing three songs for a First National comedy starring Ben Lyon and Ona Munson and directed by Clarence Badger. *The Hot Heiress* was not a success, and the songs[2] went unremarked. Then came Paramount and *Love Me Tonight*, based on a play by Leopold Marchand and Paul Armont. For it, Rodgers and Hart wrote nine numbers, so brilliantly integrated into the witty script that they are all but inseparable from it; and Mamoulian at last had something which would permit him to 'combine all the elements of movement, dancing, acting, music, singing, decor, lighting' (though not yet colour). The result was one of the most enchanting musicals ever made, the Lubitsch film that Lubitsch was always trying to pull off but never quite did.

Mamoulian's critics have always tended to dismiss *Love Me Tonight* as a pallid imitation of Lubitsch and Clair. It is possible that there was an influence, though in the case of Clair it seems to be limited to a shot or two of Paris streets and rooftops, and of Lubitsch, to the general air of sophistication and the presence of Maurice Chevalier and Jeanette MacDonald, his ineffable stars from *The Love Parade*. If so, Mamoulian in any case left his masters far behind. Dialogue exchanges like Charlie Ruggles's 'Can you go for a doctor?' and Myrna Loy's lightning 'Certainly, bring him right in!'; stylistic tricks like the sudden cut into slow motion as the castle settles down for yet another exciting evening of bridge; sounds like the extraordinary whimper, neither human nor

yet quite canine, made by the three old aunts at moments of stress; all are handled by Mamoulian with a deft, airy legerdemain which makes the famed Lubitsch touch fall like a dull thud. Indeed, to compare the finale of *Love Me Tonight* (Jeanette MacDonald racing on horseback through the fields to stand defiantly on the railway line in order to halt the train carrying Chevalier away from her) with that of *Monte Carlo* (Jeanette MacDonald on the train singing 'Beyond the Blue Horizon' as she is whisked away to happiness) is to make one wonder whether Lubitsch saw the joke. Both films build to a climactic flurry of Russian montage (horses' hooves and train wheels, flashing rails and peasants singing in the fields) – but where Mamoulian's is a delicious parody, Lubitsch's is merely a romantic pastiche. Possibly it is simply a question of taste; but after *Love Me Tonight*, both *The Love Parade* and *Monte Carlo* seem to carry their sophistication and charm with all the subtlety of a huge Germanic wink.

There are several reasons why *Love Me Tonight* stands so head-and-shoulders above any other musical for years – perhaps until the emergence of Minnelli – quite apart from the excellence of its script (by Samuel Hoffenstein again, in collaboration with Waldemar Young and George Marion, Jr) and its songs. One is the delight Mamoulian always takes in having the unlikeliest actors sing in their own voices – Walter Huston in *Summer Holiday*, for instance; apart from the rare pleasure it affords of hearing Sir C. Aubrey Smith warbling and (almost) dancing the roguish 'Mimi', this habit gives what is unashamedly a fairy-tale fantasy a kind of doggy matter-of-factness which prevents it from taking off irrevocably into the thin air of whimsy like Lubitsch's Ruritanian romances. Another is the skill with which Mamoulian interleaves songs and action, so that unlike all the contemporary musicals made by Lloyd Bacon, Busby Berkeley, Mark Sandrich or Robert Z. Leonard, one does not have the equivalent of the theatrical *trois coups* each time a production number is imminent. Most of all, though, it is – yet again – Mamoulian's impeccable feeling for rhythm and movement. In a very real sense, *Love Me Tonight* is one long, unbroken production number.

For instance: the 'Isn't It Romantic?' number near the beginning of the film grows initially out of a conversation between tailor Maurice Courtelin (Maurice Chevalier) and his customer Emile (the portly, amiable Bert Roach),

Love Me Tonight: Maurice Chevalier's 'Poor Apache'

for whom he has just made a wedding suit. Emile emerges from the fitting-room in raptures, and the conversation slips easily into doggerel rhyme:

EMILE: It's beautiful! ... It's a work of art.
MAURICE: The tailor's art / For your sweetheart.
EMILE: It's like poetry in a book! How beautiful I look!
MAURICE: The love song of the needle / Is united with the thread.
          The romance of the season ...
EMILE: / So clear that I could wed.
MAURICE: Isn't it romantic?

and as easily from this into Chevalier singing 'Isn't It Romantic?' while Emile admires himself. Then Emile, preparing to leave and suddenly remembering his stick, picks up the tune (but not the words) and sings:

Isn't it romantic? da da da da da ... a very catchy strain.
Isn't it romantic? ... Oh, I forgot my cane!

Outside, Emile turns down a taxi, preferring to walk in his new finery, and the taxi driver catches the theme from him while picking up another client ('Isn't it romantic? ... At last I've got a fare'). His fare is a musician who listens all ears ('Isn't it romantic? ... I think I'll take that down') before being dropped at the station. On the train the musician busily composes, overheard by soldiers on leave who take up the theme; cut to a troop of marching soldiers appearing over the skyline in full-throated chorus, overheard by a passing gipsy violinist who rushes off excitedly; cut again to the violinist playing the theme at a gipsy camp in the forest.

Difficult as it is to convey the subtlety with which music, dialogue and action are interwoven here (along with a deliciously funny parody of both musical and film styles), the sequence is worth attempting to describe in detail because it is typical of the infallible grace and infallible invention Mamoulian brings to the problem of *total* choreography. And the momentum isn't running out yet by a long chalk. From the gipsy encampment in the wood (by now, in a transition one barely notices, it is night), the camera pans round to a vast Gothic castle, and dissolves to Princess Jeanette (Jeanette MacDonald) embarking on a tender soprano version of the song on the moonlit balcony, rudely interrupted as the top of a ladder thumps on to the ledge beside her, and the Count de Savignac (Charles Butterworth) appears like a mooncalf for the first of a series of marvellously idiotic, silly-ass conversations studded with the many double entendres (again pre-1934 Production Code sanctions) which enliven the dialogue:

PRINCESS: Count! I'm going to bed!

COUNT: I just came up to join you.

PRINCESS: Join me!

COUNT: Join you in a little chat before dinner.

PRINCESS: Not tonight. I've had another fainting spell and my uncle the Duke thought
    bed was the best place for me.

COUNT: I always think that. … I brought along my flute hoping to entertain.

A moment later the ladder overbalances, and a despairing cry of 'Oh! I'll never be able to use it again' is heard from below. And to the Princess's solicitous query, 'Oh, Count, did you break your leg?', comes the superb reply, 'No, I fell flat on my flute.'

Having thus linked the virile tailor and the languishing princess whose paths have yet to cross in one soaring sweep through time, space and the language of music, the momentum continues in a preparation for, not only the inevitability, but the therapeutic necessity of their meeting. The opening sequence of the film, shading into the 'Isn't It Romantic?' number, was the pure exhilaration of the 'Symphony of Noises' from *Porgy*, already described in the Introduction (p. 6): a joyous hedge-hop through the streets of Paris as the city comes alive, its sounds and its people set about the business of a new day, the camera noses through a window to a solitary straw hat – Chevalier's hat – hanging on a wall, and Maurice sings the 'Song of Paree' before striding off to the accompaniment of 'How Are You?' to open up his shop. Now we are introduced to a citadel of sleep.

A swift cut from the fallen Count and his ladder takes us to a rooftop eyrie in the castle, zooming in slowly to three old ladies (the aunts) huddled round a

cauldron like Macbeth's witches, casting shadows on the wall (of course) as they cast spells invoking health for poor Princess Jeanette. From there we are whisked in to a ground-floor window where the Duke (Sir C. Aubrey Smith) rules his kingdom with a benevolent rod of iron. He crushes the hopes of his man-mad niece (Myrna Loy), leaving her sulkily muttering 'Can't we *ever* get a footman under forty in this place?'; he sternly admonishes his nephew (Charlie Ruggles) – who happens to owe Maurice a large sum for tailoring – refusing to give him any money to squander in Paris; and he settles down happily to arrange the schedule of entertainment for his guests. 'Bridge at three. Dinner at eight. And after dinner' (a stroke of inspiration), 'Bridge!' Pause. 'And what are the guests doing now?' – 'Playing Bridge, Your Grace.' Possibly it is the mixture of surprise and delight in the Duke's purring 'Ah!' that makes the sudden cut into slow motion (usually a ponderous trick) so effective; at any rate, the dead march through the bridge room, with footmen tiptoeing delicately past as though afraid to waken the somnolent players out of their suspended animation, is both wonderfully funny and a superb metaphor for what ails the Princess.

Love Me Tonight: the aunts in their eyrie

Where one has a Sleeping Beauty, one must also have a Prince Charming. And in quick succession Mamoulian takes us back to the eyrie where the three old aunts are busily conjuring a knight on a white charger, and back to Paris, where a fairy godmother, in the person of the Credit Manager of the Association of Retail Merchants, promptly obliges. Learning that the Vicomte de Vareze (Charlie Ruggles, that is) never pays his bills, his creditors appoint Maurice as their representative, with instructions to collect their money in person at the château. From there on everything is plain sailing (and sailing is the word as Mamoulian skims through the plot with incredible vivacity and invention) as Maurice meets, woos, and after a spot of bother about their different stations in life, marries his Princess.

It seems that Mamoulian recorded the entire musical score before he started shooting: hence the almost uncanny harmony between sound and image. On Maurice's arrival at the château, for instance, the place is deserted since the guests are on an outing in the forest and the footmen are playing football against the old soldiers' home. To funereal tones echoing the dead march of the bridge game, he pushes the door open on the vast, empty hallway; as he explores, the music quickens, bouncing into an accentuated chord each time he opens a door, accompanying him *presto* as he races up a series of staircases to the top of the château, trilling happily as he skips down again, and finally lapsing into the dead march as the guests return from their outing a moment or two before he reaches the hallway again. Entirely unforced in their counterpoint, the images are a perfect complement to the music, and vice versa.

Similarly, the hunt scene is turned almost into a pastoral ballet by Mamoulian's camera, which orchestrates the movements of horses and hounds through the woods in tempo with the music, even reserving a gay little theme (something Disney later copied, to vulgar effect) for the stag as it hops daintily and unconcernedly along, obviously enjoying itself hugely and oblivious to the hunting horns and baying hounds which have been momentarily suspended from the soundtrack. Later, in one of the most magical moments of the film, Maurice rescues the stag and the amused Duke orders the huntsmen to 'Go back, quickly and quietly. On tiptoe'; and in slow motion, amid a momentary hush, the horses turn and literally steal back the way they came.

Love Me Tonight: the discovery that the son of a gun is nothing but a tailor

Far from reducing the film to a predictable pattern, this annotation of (and by) the music in fact gives Mamoulian complete freedom to indulge his fantasy without losing his bearings. I have already described the way 'Isn't It Romantic?' was used to bridge space and time, but perhaps the most striking example is the 'Son of a Gun is Nothing But a Tailor' number, which also disposes of the entire plot crisis with maximum effect and minimum fuss in a single song. The sequence begins upstairs in the château as Maurice finally confesses to the Princess that he is not a baron but a humble tailor, and the three aunts rush yapping and squeaking downstairs, burst into the drawing room with the news, and knock over a vase which crashes to the floor with a deafening explosion. Consternation among the guests revolving round the Duke as the social crisis reverberates; silence; then slowly, a magnificent, agonised 'Ohhhh! ... A tailor!!!!' from the Duke as he launches into the song. Then a superb overhead shot of the hallway outside shows the footmen spreading out star-fashion, each to a door, and carrying the news to the depths of the château where the song is taken up in turn by butler, valet, chambermaid, chef and washerwoman; a shot of the Princess in her room, sorrowfully muttering 'Nothing but a tailor!'; and finally, in a low-angled shot from somewhere under the generous curve of the butler's stomach, Maurice runs the gauntlet of a line of supercilious footmen whispering 'the son of a gun is nothing but a tailor' as the song ends and he ignominiously takes his leave of the château.

With the exception of 'Poor Apache', sung cabaret-fashion by Chevalier to entertain the guests at the château (and ending with a typical visual coup – seen in shadow on the wall – as he nods his head violently and his cap falls off to illustrate the guillotining of the 'poor Apache'), all the songs are used with the same playful unpredictability; and this is undoubtedly why Mamoulian is able to adhere faithfully to the conventions of the time – at the same time sending them up – without ever becoming bogged down by them. The romantic climax when Maurice lures the Princess out into the garden during the ball, for instance, is almost archetypal. Moonlight dapples the blossom on the trees as the lovers sit gazing into each other's eyes and the music starts up dreamily: a cue since time immemorial for a romantic duet. Instead, Mamoulian plays the scene on dialogue, and only when the lovers have gone severally to bed does he unite them in song in their dreams, with a split screen placing them

side by side on the pillows as their voices soar into the title song, 'Love Me Tonight'.

Rodgers and Hart, of course, provide a wonderful springboard with their brilliant music and lyrics, but the wit and flourish of *Love Me Tonight* are uniquely Mamoulian's own. Even the impeccable cast are handled like instruments in an orchestra, so that the chirruping aunts, gruff Sir Aubrey Smith, manhunting Myrna Loy, Robert Greig's sonorous butler, and the twin gloom and irrepressibility of Charles Butterworth and Charlie Ruggles, are woven like recurring motifs into the texture, whose main purpose is a merciless send-up of the immaculately conceived heroine of convention. The Princess, we are told, is wasting away like Camille from an unknown malady. But the doctor who examines her with a rather less than professional eye, leaves us in no doubt as to his diagnosis: 'You're not wasting away,' he pronounces. 'You're just wasted.' And Maurice, to her unutterable outrage, offers an unmistakable

Love Me Tonight: Jeanette MacDonald and Maurice Chevalier

cure when he looks her straight in the eye to sing 'You know I'd like to have a little son of Mimi by-and-by'.

Tipped out of the carriage in which she has been bowling along gaily singing 'Lover' and dumped unceremoniously in a ditch; responding with a soft, hurt 'Oh!' of indignation as she reproves her lover for ungentlemanly conduct only to be told 'And you, Your Highness, are not a woman'; subjected to the indignity of Chevalier's look of silent incredulity as he measures her for a riding habit and records a modest 34 inches for bust – Jeanette MacDonald cheerfully aids and abets her own destruction in one of her most enchanting performances. Her heroic finale, when she casts discretion and social consideration aside and gallops across the fields in an Eisensteinian montage of hooves and train wheels to stand on the track, arms akimbo and head thrown proudly back as the train (and her lover) rushes towards her, is – like *Love Me Tonight* itself – an ineffable mixture of absurdity and enchantment.

5: *Song of Songs*

Marlene Dietrich had just made her fifth film in a row with Josef von Sternberg. *Blonde Venus* was not the success hoped for after *Shanghai Express*, and both Paramount and Sternberg – though not, apparently, Dietrich – felt it was time for a change. The result was *Song of Songs*, a curious and rather endearing mixture of Sternbergian splendour and Mamoulian send-up. Sandwiched as it is in the great crescendo of seven Sternberg films running from *The Blue Angel* to *The Devil is a Woman*, it has been unjustly neglected – perhaps because Mamoulian allowed the Goddess to descend from Olympus, to exist rather than simply to *be*.

Whatever role she played, Sternberg's Dietrich was quintessentially a love goddess, a statue brought to life to wreak her havoc with infinite subtlety but within certain preordained lines of grace, beauty and mystery. In *Dishonored*, for instance, her characterisations as prostitute and peasant girl are mere masquerades pending the emergence of the enigmatic Mata Hari who will ultimately walk out to meet the firing squad as coolly and gracefully as if to an amorous tryst. As Andrew Sarris puts it: 'The grave deliberateness and delicate grace with which Dietrich plies her trade as a prostitute gives the show away from the very beginning. In no other film does Dietrich so self-consciously try on different roles for size and style. Her fantasy prostitute is no less committed than her fake peasant to the service of a love which transcends the trivial issues of politics.'

The deliberation and grace are still there when she makes her first appearance in *Song of Songs* as the humble peasant girl, Lily, taking leave of her father's grave and sped on her way by a patriarchal sexton as she picks up her little bundle of worldly goods and walks off through a blossom-laden orchard to seek her fortune in Berlin. The difference is that her characterisation is allowed to take root and develop, with perfect conviction and credibility, from innocence to awareness and then disillusion, until finally we are again face to face with the Sternberg Dietrich, the goddess who knows all things of all men.

Mamoulian, of course, must have been only too aware that it was asking a lot to expect audiences to accept Lola-Lola/Shanghai Lily as a shy, unspoiled virgin. Cunningly, therefore, he undercuts disbelief by surrounding the character with outward trappings of humour and an undertow of sensuality. When she arrives at her Aunt Rasmussen's home in Berlin, Lily is encased in voluminous mourning with an enormous cartwheel hat perched precariously on the back of her demure braids. Truculent Aunt Rasmussen (Alison Skipworth) promptly packs her off to bed, snappishly urging her to 'Take that black pancake off your head and climb out of that shroud', and watching in amazement as Lily peels off her dress and three petticoats and still remains amply covered. Left alone, Lily gazes dreamily out of the window, then retires to bed with her Bible, and begins to read – from the 'Song of Solomon'. 'By night on my bed I sought him whom my soul loveth. I sought him but I found him not. I will rise now, and go about the city. In the streets and in the broad ways I will seek him whom my soul loveth.'

With the thin ice thus safely negotiated, Mamoulian has no difficulty with the charming sex comedy of the scenes in which Lily meets and bewitches her soul-mate from the 'Song of Solomon' – a sculptor, Richard Waldow (Brian Aherne), who is inspired by a glimpse of her leg as she decorates a ladder in her aunt's bookshop and who lures her to his studio to pose for him. Easily and wittily, Mamoulian sketches in the theme of the birth of love and the appearance of the canker in the rose as the first bloom is lost. On her first visit to the studio, Lily sneaks out fearfully, hesitates on the threshold, and is appalled to see Richard's imaginary sketch of herself ('Oh! I haven't any clothes on!'), but nevertheless allows herself to be coaxed into posing, bashfully and blushingly, in the nude. As she leaves, she encounters the monocled, moustachioed and evidently depraved Baron von Merzbach (Lionel Atwill), who has commissioned the statue and mutters 'Lovely gel … she

interests me *very* much ... very much', as he blows a defiling cloud of cigarette smoke over her sketch. 'She means nothing to me,' says Richard.

On her next visit (some time later), Lily is no longer the innocent, and laces Aunt Rasmussen's nightcap with an additional tot of rum before running upstairs and into the studio, gay and self-assured. In an extraordinarily erotic scene, Richard, troubled by Lily and by a block in his inspiration, irritatedly massages the statue's shoulders, then seizes her to correct her pose. Inevitably, they kiss. Fade out and in to an idyllic scene of the couple in a rowing boat; dappling sunlight, weeping willows drooping into the water, Lily radiant in straw hat and white dress picked out with flowers; they race away across a hill.

Stunningly shot by Victor Milner, the sequence has a genuine, urgent lyricism, reminiscent of the romantic idyll between the Prince and Mitzi in the apple orchard in Stroheim's *The Wedding March*. The comparison is not fortuitous, since it is to Stroheim rather than Sternberg that the film now turns in three scenes detailing the process of corruption. Firstly, the Baron arrives in Aunt Rasmussen's bookshop to bargain in a gentlemanly way:

Song of Songs: first visit to the studio. Marlene Dietrich as Lily

BARON: Let's not beat about the bush, Frau Rasmussen. I have a library, a very extensive library, and I require someone to take care of it; someone familiar with books. Your niece could do it very well.

AUNT: My niece, Excellency?

BARON: She would have to live at my place. I am prepared to pay her a very liberal salary.

AUNT: Why, Excellency ... [*laughs*] ... my niece could hardly ... uh ...

BARON: All the proprieties would be observed.

AUNT: Still, Excellency ... [*laughs*] ... a young girl in a bachelor's household?

BARON: Hmmm! A very rare edition. A thousand marks? [*It is priced at 3 marks.*] That's a lot of money for a book. Understand me, Frau Rasmussen, when I set my mind upon a thing, I usually get it, one way or another.

AUNT: Perhaps your Excellency would be interested in my other books?

BARON: Yes, no doubt, no doubt. I shall be dropping in from time to time. Let me see, what were we talking about? Oh, yes, your niece ...

A dissolve takes us in to the second scene: Lily pirouetting gaily under the trees. Falling beside Richard, she presses her face to the earth, begging him to smell it. Lily soars radiantly into a breathless declaration of her love: 'When I put my hands on the earth, it's you I'm touching. The wind on my face is your kisses. You are in everything I think and feel and do, and will be till I die.' But as she talks of their love, he talks only of their possible separation. Lily refuses to listen: 'Set me as a seal upon thine heart, as a seal upon thine arm. For love is strong as death.' Fade out and in – on a shot of the completed statue in the studio – to the third scene, where Richard complains to the Baron about the mess he is in with no money, a career to make, and Lily expecting him to marry her. 'Give her to me,' says the Baron, 'I can make her happy and you won't.'

With its graceful narrative and free-flowing transitions, the film has so far been perfect Mamoulian, notable for the complex symbolism which grows up round the statue. Lily has already named it during her first visit to the studio: 'The girl in the Song of Songs ... She's the girl who feels in her heart that somewhere the perfect love is waiting for her. ... It is the voice of my beloved.' As the statue draws near to completion, it enshrines the impossible purity of Lily's dream; and when Lily comes to the studio to find Richard gone and the

Song of Songs: Marlene Dietrich

Song of Songs: the Baron (Lionel Atwill) awaits … and Lily after the fall

Baron waiting for her, it has been covered by a dustsheet, ready for the removal men.

The trouble with the last third of the film – Lily's corruption and regeneration – is that it really needs a director with Stroheim's cruelty as well as Stroheim's tenderness. Wielding the scalpel has never been Mamoulian's forte, and although the sequences after Lily's marriage to the Baron are done with his usual impeccable style, something is lacking. A touch of moral and emotional ambiguity, perhaps, as Lily becomes the dark avenger and the Baron, who genuinely loves her, is made to suffer what she has suffered. Somehow the contradictory elements which Stroheim fuses together so easily, here remain obstinately apart: the discarded mistress hovering demonically in the background; the Baron brushing up his moustache, perfuming his breast, screwing in his monocle and taking a last puff of his cigarette before strutting off (the image of a Stroheim prince) to Lily's bedroom on their wedding-night; the handsome young steward making desperately inviting sheep's eyes at the new lady of the manor. When the Baron finally invites Richard to inspect the masterpiece he has, Pygmalion-like, made of Lily, his increasing agitation as he gradually realises that they are still in love somehow gets only the drunken ecstasy and none of the agony. And the aftermath – Lily revenging herself on both men by repairing to a lodge in the garden, hurling herself into the amazed and rapturous steward's arms, knocking over a lamp with her dress so that the lodge bursts into flames, and finally stalking away into the night (like Amy Jolly disappearing into the desert in *Morocco*) as the Baron frantically brandishes his gun – blows up into amiable and highly enjoyable absurdity.

Thereafter Sternberg's Dietrich makes a brief but welcome appearance as Lily becomes a sultry, smoky nightclub singer, entertaining elderly gentlemen and singing the sexy 'Johnny' ('I need a kiss or two, or maybe more'), as Richard enters. He persuades her to come back to the studio with him, and as he lights the lamp, Lily is revealed in her black dress standing beneath the dazzling white statue. A shot of her face in close-up, startled by its purity. She controls herself, crosses to the pillar where she was first persuaded to undress for the sculpture, and asks for a cigarette. Close-up of the statue.

RICHARD: She's still the same.

LILY: She's a fool. What is she waiting for? What is she listening for?

Richard interrupts her bitter tirade, reminding her of the 'Song of Solomon', and gradually caught up by it, she begins to recite: 'I sought him whom my soul loved. I sought him, but I found him not. I called him, but he gave me no answer. The watchmen that went about the city found me. They smote me and they wounded me. The keepers of the wall took away my veil from me ...' But when Richard begs forgiveness, insisting that he still loves her, she is gripped by hysterical rage: 'Then you love somebody who's dead! I'm dead, do you hear, dead! What right has she to live?' And, seizing a hammer, she smashes the statue. As she collapses, Richard takes her in his arms and gently murmurs, 'We'll start again.'

As a finale, and as a codicil to the symbolism, the scene has an undoubted splendour. But it contains its own, possibly inadvertent, comment on the whole latter part of the film. As Dietrich seizes the hammer and smashes the statue, a reaction shot of Brian Aherne shows him looking on with an expression which can only be summed up as a shrug signifying 'Oh, well!' Possibly bad acting; but it does testify to a basic uncertainty of conception in the film, which never quite makes up its mind whether it is opting for tender lyricism, stringent mockery of human fallibility, or simply melodramatic splendour. In the event it gives a pretty good account of all three.

Song of Songs: 'What right has she to live ...'

6: *Queen Christina*

After Dietrich, who else but Garbo? Although Hollywood still quailed before Mamoulian's persistent non-conformity, his critical reputation was riding high and he was duly signed by MGM – at Garbo's personal request – to direct *Queen Christina*.

Probably no two people will ever agree as to which was Garbo's greatest role. Her films are notoriously difficult to assess anyway, since her luminous presence turns dross into gold even with silly scripts (*A Woman of Affairs*) or silly direction (*Susan Lenox: Her Fall and Rise*). But *Queen Christina* is unique in that its script is perfectly suited to, and its director perfectly understood, that peculiar Garbo mystique which Kenneth Tynan pinned down so neatly (*Sight and Sound*, April 1954): 'Tranced by the ecstasy of existing, she gives to each onlooker what he needs: her largesse is *intarissable*. Most actresses in action live only to look at men, but Garbo looks at flowers, clouds and furniture with the same admiring compassion, like Eve on the morning of creation ... In England two years ago she visited Westminster Abbey, early one morning when no one was about, and in this most public of places found a source of enormous private enchantment.' And *Queen Christina* is, precisely, the story of a woman who grows up in the belief that the world is a place of solitude, then suddenly discovers the power to communicate with its enchantment.

It is surely no accident that in the film's two most celebrated sequences – perhaps two of the most fondly remembered scenes in her entire career – Garbo appears virtually alone. The first – the famous bedroom-stroking sequence – represents the Queen's rapturous discovery that there *is* a source of enchantment in her world as she prepares to leave the room in which she has

Queen Christina: Garbo with Ian Keith and David Torrence

found love. Mamoulian has described it as a sonnet,[3] but it is really a lingering, longing caress as she drifts slowly round the room, stroking her hands gently along the surface of a sideboard, pausing at a mirror to smile at her lover's reflection, touching a box, a spinning-wheel, a wall, as though they had shared some secret with her, closing her eyes to remember, then continuing her journey, round the bed, across it to kiss the pillow, to run her fingers wonderingly over an ikon on the wall, until Antonio asks what she is doing, and that soft, throaty voice wells up from the deep: 'I have been memorising this room. In the future, in my memory, I shall live a great deal in this room.'

The second sequence, the great elegiac rite of the end, is the moment in the future she has been preparing for, when she must draw on this memory and live in it. Her lover has been killed in a duel, and as the ship that will bear them back to Spain prepares to set sail, she moves majestically to the bows. The last, magnificent close-up is held and held as she stands immobile as a figurehead, staring inscrutably ahead, remembering, until the image slowly fades. The effect is devastating, drawing on everything that has gone before and yet drawing on nothing. If one needs any further evidence of Mamoulian's intuitive understanding of Garbo's unique talent (nearly every other director who worked with her surrounded her with bustle and asked her to *do* too much), one need only read his comment on this scene: 'Garbo asked me: "What do I play in this scene?" Remember, she is standing there for 150 feet of film – 90 feet of them in close-up. I said: "Have you heard of *tabula rasa*? I want your face to be a blank sheet of paper. I want the writing to be done by every member of the audience. I'd like it if you could avoid even blinking your eyes, so that you're nothing but a beautiful mask." So in fact there is *nothing* on her face: but everyone who has seen the film will tell you what she is thinking and feeling. And always it's something different.'

Almost inevitably, perhaps, *Queen Christina* has come to be remembered as a two-sequence film, with all the rest consigned to oblivion. This is unfair. Admittedly there is some Hollywood rhubarbing among the Swedish peasantry; admittedly, too, John Gilbert looks distinctly stilted and uncomfortable in his romantic role as the Spanish ambassador who comes to woo her for his King and falls in love with her himself. Nevertheless, the script has moments of genuine distinction, besides being carefully constructed, and

Mamoulian manages to give it that easy, graceful flow which was by now well and truly established as his signature.

As usual the beginning is an impeccable piece of scene setting. A long-held shot of the royal coat of arms, accompanied on the soundtrack by a fanfare; a brief battlefield scene in which a knight in armour challenges his dying enemy – the King of Sweden – to reveal his identity; a shot of the crown and sceptre as the loyal Oxenstierna (Lewis Stone) introduces the new Queen to her Parliament, describing how the child, their future ruler, has been brought up as a boy. Brushing away his helping hand, the tiny Queen insists on clambering unaided to her throne, where she sits regally dwarfed to make her speech about the conduct of the war. 'We promise ... she concludes, then pauses, the lines gone. 'To wage it with honour,' Oxenstierna prompts. 'To WIN it,' she amends belligerently.

The cut which follows bridges some fifteen years and a lifetime of weary solitude and expectancy as Christina, now a woman, returns from the hunt to be greeted by her Parliament clamouring for her attention, clamouring for the war to continue, clamouring for their Queen to marry the national war hero, Prince Charles. The abstracted efficiency with which she deals with these affairs of state, or embraces her unprepossessing current lover, Magnus, magnificently suggests the caged freedom of a young eagle poised for flight but restrained by invisible bars. Even her concern for the peasantry and her determination to oppose her counsellors and end the war which makes her people suffer has the slightly plangent note of regal duty. When she cries 'Spoil, glory, flags, trumpets – what is behind those words? Cripples, dead men. I want for my people security and happiness. I want to cultivate the arts of happiness. I want peace, and peace I will have,' one finds little of the brooding sympathy which so often made her voice hover protectively like the folded wings of a swan over suffering humanity. For that one must wait until she is alone, communing with herself and her vision of what might be. This, after all, is the Queen who will give up her throne, her country and her people for a memory.

The key sequence, therefore, comes immediately after the signing of the peace treaty when Christina, her duty fulfilled, is once more thrust back upon her solitude. In the first light of dawn, she rises and in a moment of pure

(*next page*) *Queen Christina*: the Queen envies her lady-in-waiting. Garbo with Elizabeth Young and Edward Norris

exhilaration stands poised in the frosty air of her balcony before scooping up a handful of snow and rubbing it on her face.[4] Instead of capitalising immediately on the scene, Mamoulian returns to the peacetime tedium of the court – her glacially correct reception of the French ambassador, her despairing cry of 'Must we live for the dead?' when Oxenstierna once more tries to persuade her of the political wisdom of a marriage to Prince Charles. Then a long, lingering, magnificent close-up as she stands at the window staring out over the endless, unchanging landscape of white: 'Snow,' mourns the voice of the greatest blues singer of all, 'is like a wild sea. One could go out and get lost in it and forget the world.'

Too often in her films, insensitive direction brought Garbo to her zenith too soon, leaving her no choice but to level off. But even a meteor must fall, and now, Mamoulian's melodic sense must have warned him, was the moment. So he takes her back to square one, ready for her new voyage of discovery in search of that 'private enchantment': her chance meeting with the Spanish ambassador – neither of them aware of the other's identity – when she comes across his snowbound carriage while out hunting. Mamoulian has described how he was determined that Garbo must laugh at her first glimpse of the stranded Spaniards, and how in rehearsal she tried, she even smiled, but never really let go. Finally, in despair, Mamoulian requested a final rehearsal; secretly he asked John Gilbert and Akim Tamiroff (playing the ambassador's servant) to pull the most fiendish faces they could devise as soon as Garbo appeared; and he set the cameras rolling. The result, captured in one take, is perfect: a full-throated, uninhibited belly laugh which melts the ice and leads unerringly into the gentle *gauloiserie* of the scenes that follow as Queen and ambassador (she in hunting clothes, he believing her a boy) take shelter in a country inn which has only one available room.

Garbo handles the bantering comedy of mistaken sex and mistaken identity with such subtlety and perfect timing that one wonders why all the fuss was made about her talents as a comedienne when Lubitsch extracted a much coarser performance from her in *Ninotchka*. The mischievous pleasure she takes in settling a taproom argument about the Queen's sex life by announcing that the lady in question has had twelve lovers, and her delight in the roar of 'Long Live the Queen' which greets the slander; the well-bred bow to the inevitable with which she defers to the ambassador's insistence ('My sleeping manners are beyond reproach') that she share his room; the defiant little toss of the head, daring reproof, with which she closes the door on her elderly and outraged servant: all this reveals the touch of the born comedienne. Even better, the note of wistful eroticism which she somehow manages to sustain, felt but unheard and unseen until, with a faint smile, she takes off her doublet and waits patiently for the truth to dawn.

It is this underlying tonality of self-abandon that sends the film winging on its upward flight again, through the saraband of farewell to the room to the pure epiphany of the end. A good deal of action intervenes between these twin summits, of course: the ambassador's discovery of the identity of his lover; the fury of the populace and the jealousy of Magnus; the pressure on Christina not to marry a foreigner; her confrontation with her people; her abdication. Yet there is really no intervention: above it all rises Christina, serene and immutable in spite of approaching tragedy, secure in the discovery she made when,

hugging herself with secret joy after completing her tour of the room, she murmured: 'This is how the Lord must have felt when he beheld the finished world with all his creatures, loving, breathing.' Christina disposes of her kingdom, her life and her love, and like God on the Seventh Day, has no more to do but contemplate her creation and see that it is well. When she arrives on board the ship that was to carry them to Spain, she kneels beside her lover, mortally wounded in a duel with Magnus. He dies, she pulls her cloak about her face, and moves almost with exaltation into the bows to face the warm winds and sun of Spain he promised, her serenity barely rippled by a grief that is itself almost tranquil in its acceptance of inevitability.

Curiously enough, in spite of their many radical differences, the film that comes most stubbornly to mind in connection with *Queen Christina* is Sternberg's *Scarlet Empress*. On the face of it, nothing could be more dissimilar than the controlled introspection of Garbo and the extrovert extravagance of

Queen Christina: 'tabula rasa …'

Dietrich; the way Mamoulian isolates his Queen against wastes of snow and barren stonework, while Sternberg drenches his Empress in baroque statuary and glittering pomp; the essentially true emotions of Christina and the theatrical inflations of Catherine. Yet, as Eric H. Rideout has pointed out (*The American Film*, Mitre Press, 1937), *Queen Christina* presents a 'credible, romantic and inaccurate view of Sweden', while *The Scarlet Empress* is 'a fantastic yet essentially accurate picture'. And when one is finally confronted by the triumph of sensuality over circumstance in both Queen and Empress – Christina immobile on the prow of her ship, Catherine exultant on her throne – fantasy and reality are inextricably mingled, with the visions of both directors invading the same no man's land of the creative imagination.

7: *We Live Again*

Continuing his run as a ladies' director to rival George Cukor, Mamoulian next took on Anna Sten, the Ukrainian actress whom Samuel Goldwyn brought to Hollywood from Berlin after seeing her in Ozep's remarkable early sound version of *The Murder of Dmitri Karamazov*, convinced that he had discovered a major star. Although he gave up trying to prove his point after spending a fortune on three films[5] – *Nana*, *We Live Again* (both 1934) and *The Wedding Night* (1935) – which left the public profoundly indifferent, Goldwyn's talent-spotting instincts had not really betrayed him. I have not seen King Vidor's *The Wedding Night*, but in *Nana*, Sten's acting is much the most interesting feature of a film which has been romanticised out of all resemblance to Zola's original and directed by Dorothy Arzner as a fluffy plod; and in *We Live Again* her performance is again excellent, revealing much the same sort of warm, robust fragility as the early Ingrid Bergman.

Following the miscalculations of *Nana*, Goldwyn decided to give his Russian protégée a Russian ambiance, and *We Live Again*, based on Tolstoy's drama of sin and regeneration, *Resurrection*, is something of a sentimental journey for Mamoulian too – the only film he ever made which really betrays his origins. Of course *We Live Again* does not portray a real Russia any more than *Queen Christina* presented an historical Sweden; but the atmosphere so perfectly captures that peculiar Russian dichotomy – a dark night of the soul matched with an exquisitely luminous daylight of the senses – that for once one is not embarrassed by a Hollywood attempt to deal with Tolstoy's revolutionary ardours and peasant simplicities. From the outset one is translated into the feel and smell of an alien land in a montage of eight brief, low-angled shots which effortlessly capture the glistening, sensuous lustre of Dovzhenko's vision of a new, burgeoning land:

1. Shot of trees in blossom against sky; rich, warm, dappling sunlight. Dissolve to
2. Closer shot. Dissolve to
3. Field seen through a blossom-laden branch in the foreground. Dissolve to
4. Field with bullock on skyline. Dissolve to
5. Rivulet, horses grazing in distance. Dissolve to
6. Ploughing in field. Dissolve to
7. Skyline. Three horses and ploughs appearing over horizon in a row. Dissolve to
8. Close-up of each of three women behind the ploughs, sowing the field.

Underlying this heroic pastorale lies a quiet glint of humour. Nothing tangible, simply a hint that the horses appearing in unison over the skyline might at any moment take their bow like well-drilled chorines; but it leads

We Live Again: love in the farmyard (Fredric March and Anna Sten)

smoothly into the flurry and bustle surrounding the return of Prince Dmitri (Fredric March) as Katusha (Anna Sten), alerted in the barnyard, rushes upstairs to change, forgetting that she has a piglet in her arms, and somehow still carrying it when they meet in the hall, thrusts it into Dmitri's arms in order to make her curtsy. Never fond of solemnity at the best of times, Mamoulian makes the most of the pair of chattering aunts (reminiscent, though diminished, of the trio from *Love Me Tonight*), and of the ritual greeting of the lord of the manor by his serfs. Embarrassed by the gifts they heap on him, which in his revolutionary fervour he feels they need more than he does, Dmitri insists on thanking them personally (to everybody's consternation). 'Friends,' he begins with an expansive gesture, dropping the loaf he is clutching and ending the attempt at fraternisation.

The same gentle humour, again with the same earthy, sunlit feel about Gregg Toland's superb camerawork, pervades the dreamy, enchanted

We Live Again: the Dovzhenko look

atmosphere of the scenes that follow as Dmitri and Katusha pursue their innocent, adolescent romance – she milking her cows, he urging equality of the people and crossly muttering, 'Katusha, you're only beautiful, not bright', as she confounds him by asking who will do the work when everybody is equal. Scarcely touched by rumblings from the aunts that of course a prince can't actually *marry* a peasant girl, they pursue their idyll of pure romance in balmy, summer hours, sealing all their differences with a kiss amid the shady, secluded branches of their private tree.

The difficulty, obviously, in reducing Tolstoy's novel to an 84-minute film is how to make Dmitri's change of heart and subsequent behaviour credible: not merely his summary abandonment of revolutionary principles when he rejoins his regiment (they could, after all, be explained away as adolescent enthusiasm), but his seduction of Katusha on his return two years later, which should be inspired as much by love as by lust (otherwise his

We Live Again: the Easter Mass (Fredric March and Anna Stern)

subsequent agony of remorse is without adequate foundation). Mamoulian solves the first problem quite well in a series of brief scenes where Dmitri is encouraged by brother officers to flirt with senior regimental wives in the interests of promotion, begins to enjoy a life of elegant debauch, and finally lights a cigarette from a leaf casually torn from the revolutionary tract which has been his Bible. But his real triumph is over the second, emotional, problem.

It is Easter when Dmitri returns from the army two years later, responding with casual affection to Katusha's unchanged adoration. Almost immediately they set off for church in a magnificent evocation of the celebration of the Easter Mass, which, as a contemporary reviewer commented, featured half the Russian exiles in America, plus a Tolstoy or two. The glittering procession of ikons, incense, candles, wrinkled faces and patriarchal beards builds into a paean of adoration as the Gregorian chant rings out and the rite of the Easter kiss begins. Two shots, close-ups, of Dmitri and Katusha facing each other; the cry of 'Christ is Risen' is answered by the ritual 'He is indeed'; and, as they kiss, in that moment their love is reborn.

The seduction scene which follows is equally brilliantly handled, with subtle shifts and reversals of photographic textures dovetailing the two moods of the film. It begins, as the household prepares for bed, with an exterior shot of the house, the lights extinguished one by one, leaving only two windows illuminated. The tone changes to a soft, moonlit glow in a lovely shot of Katusha sitting in her bedroom behind a billowing gauze curtain, dreamily plaiting her hair as Dmitri appears in the garden and persuades her to go for a walk. 'Do you remember our tree?' she asks. 'Shall we go there?' Instead he leads her to a greenhouse in the orchard where, touched by his love and trapped by his passionate pleas ('I might get killed.... It is you who have changed, not I'), she yields. They kiss, and in what looks like a return to the pathetic fallacy of *City Streets*, rain starts beating down; but after a shot of the rain dripping off the roof, of a candle-lit ikon, Mamoulian dissolves to a bright, cloudless morning as Dmitri, back in his own room and framed against a sun-streaked window where purring doves hover, prepares to steal away to his regiment before Katusha wakens. Time passes tranquilly, the aunts chatter about Katusha's condition, and two tiny, perfect scenes plunge the film into the

(*previous page*) *We Live Again*: the seduction scene

darkness of Katusha's ruin and despair: she runs after a train, desperately trying to attract Dmitri's attention as he plays cards inside, and slips on the dark, rain-soaked platform as the train pulls out; accompanied only by an old, black-robed servant, she struggles over the hillside with her baby's coffin to the unconsecrated ground where it must be buried.

Cut to Moscow, seven years later. A richly laden table, footmen, music, Dmitri – now bearded – dancing with the aristocratic Missy (Jane Baxter), daughter of Prince Kortchagin (Sir C. Aubrey Smith). 'People will begin to think you're marrying me because you love me,' he says teasingly. Despite the easy transition, the second half of the film – the regeneration – is not really satisfactory. There is something much too coincidental, for instance, about the way Dmitri and Katusha are thrown together again (he is invited by Kortchagin to act as juryman on a case he is trying, and Katusha, charged with murder, is the accused), and something much too fortuitous about the way Katusha is strenuously shown to be not guilty but is condemned on a point of procedure to five years' hard labour in Siberia. These faults belong to Tolstoy and the script-writers, of course, but Mamoulian seems somehow to have lost his impetus anyway. The jail scenes are embarrassingly bad, depicting a sort of female Alcatraz where hard-boiled molls scrap, knock back the vodka, and exchange such confidences as 'What did they get you for?' So ill-matched are these scenes that they seem like the work of another director.

Only slightly less unhappy are the trial scenes, involving some laboured comedy with the ruffianly but lovable couple (well played by Dale Fuller and Leonid Kinsky) who stand accused with Katusha; while the notion of casting two very English players as the aristocratic Kortchagins comes to grief in Jane Baxter's performance of appalling, lisping Kensingtonian prissiness. All this part of the film, in fact, is a long, muddled hiatus which obscures the main line with details which are both naïve and unnecessary, such as Katusha's encounter with a political prisoner who happens to be the author of the revolutionary pamphlet which inspired Dmitri, or Dmitri's sudden rediscovery of his beliefs through Missy's sneers ('Dear, dear, he's gone socialist'). Isolated moments stand out: the lovers, separated by two grilles with guards patrolling between them, trying to make themselves heard over the babble of voices in the prison; Katusha's agony when she realises that Dmitri is trying to help her and cries:

'Something terrible is happening to me. I'm coming alive.' But the film only recovers its momentum, moving from the spring and brief summer of their love into its long winter, with the magnificent sequence of Dmitri's resurrection.

Alone in his room, Dmitri stares at a framed photograph of himself taken years before. His face freezes on the screen; superimposed are memories of his seduction of Katusha, his voice saying 'It is you who have changed, not I.' He wanders round the room, abstractedly picks out a few notes on the piano, then sits down and begins to play; the music swells, superimposed is the Easter ceremony, he and Katusha kissing. Weeping, he rises, pauses at an ikon on the wall, kneels to pray: 'Dear Heavenly Father, give me courage, I have so much to do. So many wrongs to right. Give me courage not to fail. Help me, dear God, to live again.' Then, rising, he moves slowly to the window. The elements may be unpromisingly conventional, but out of them Mamoulian has fashioned

We Live Again: resurrection begins

a snowball of emotion as momentous as the bedroom-stroking in *Queen Christina*, revealing not only the depth of Dmitri's remorse but also – a tremor of doubt after his prayer, a slight hesitancy in his pose at the window – his misgivings as to the honesty of his resolution to 'save his soul' by marrying Katusha. Furiously rejected by her, he finds the courage to strip himself of his pride and his possessions, and follows her to Siberia.

In spite of its weaknesses – only the haunting mask of a Garbo might have dominated the later prolixities – *We Live Again* remains remarkable for its first half, as well as for Toland's photography and the performances of Anna Sten and Fredric March. All things considered, too, it is remarkable how much of Tolstoy Mamoulian has managed to preserve in what was obviously designed to be consumed as a romance with a happy ending. At the end, in a bleak snowscape dominated by the vast obelisk which marks the boundary to Siberia, Dmitri overtakes the weary, ragged prisoners on their march. 'You have come *here?*' asks Katusha. Dmitri explains how he has given up everything to follow her: 'All I ask is to live again with your forgiveness and your help and your love.' The music swells encouragingly as they march off into the unknown together; but Katusha, echoing Tolstoy's conception of the bitter ashes of true resurrection, is saying, 'I am not the Katusha you once knew.'

8: *Becky Sharp*

However natural the circumstance may now seem, it was only by accident that Mamoulian came to direct *Becky Sharp*, the first feature in the new three-colour Technicolor process. Pioneer Pictures, a company formed by Merian C. Cooper, John Hay Whitney and Cornelius V. Whitney to launch this Technicolor process in live-action films (it had been used for some time in Disney cartoons), had made a very successful start in July 1934, with a short film, *La Cucaracha*, designed by Robert Edmond Jones and directed by Lloyd Corrigan; and a rather less successful continuation with the colour sequences interpolated into *The House of Rothschild* and *Kid Millions*. On 3 December shooting began on *Becky Sharp* under the direction of Lowell Sherman, Garbo's leading man in *The Divine Woman*, who had turned director in 1930. On 28 December, Sherman died. On 14 January 1935 shooting started again – from scratch and with the script partly rewritten – with Mamoulian in charge. The result, designed overall by Robert Edmond Jones, is still a strikingly beautiful film, using colour as delicately as Wedgwood china; and it may also lay a reasonable claim to being the first film to have used colour throughout to dramatic rather than decorative ends.

The most celebrated example is also the most obvious: the Duchess of Richmond's great ball on the eve of Waterloo, when the blues, greens and yellows are gradually drained away to leave the screen suffused by a crescendo of red. The sequence begins with an ominous shot of Napoleon on horseback, seen in silhouette against a wall, over which the first shot of the ball is superimposed. Lovely overhead shots of the dancers swirling across the ornate, blue-patterned floor; brilliant flashes of colour as Becky, surrounded by

scarlet-coated officers, flits from Joseph Sedley to George Osborne, from insulting Lady Bareacres to scraping an acquaintance with the Marquis of Steyne. Meanwhile, in the soft moonlight of the balcony, Dobbin consoles Amelia, promising to send her husband to her. As she waits forlornly, she is joined by an elderly gentleman who proves to be the Duke of Wellington, talking gloomily of a night which may end all too soon. 'What's over there?' asks Amelia, gazing at the horizon; and the reply, 'A French village. Waterloo, they call it,' is answered by a slow, ominous rumbling in the distance. Inside the ballroom, the dancers hover, suspended momentarily as voices fearfully mutter 'Cannon? ... Thunder? ... Artillery?' The dance begins again, there is a second rumble, louder, and again the dancers freeze. With the third rumble, the windows burst open, the curtains billow over the dancefloor, extinguishing the lights, and flashes of gunfire on the skyline illuminate the scene of panic as first the ladies, then the men, and finally the military – drenching the screen in a sea of scarlet cloaks – evacuate the ballroom.

Becky Sharp: the Waterloo Ball. Cedric Hardwicke and Miriam Hopkins

In the prints currently available of the film, the sequence is somewhat garbled by cuts and missing frames, but some idea of its original state – and Mamoulian's intentions – may be gleaned from the following extract from an article he wrote in *Picturegoer*, 13 July 1935:

It is a sequence in which dialogue is of no moment. Were I picturing it in black-and-white, I would have contrast in photography, composition, angles and tempo with which to build up the effect. In colour, one additional and very important means is available to me.

Colour, as you know, is symbolic. It is not an accident that traffic stop lights are red, go lights green. Red means danger, green safety and hope.

So in the first few shots of this sequence, the people who run by the camera are dressed in cool colours, starting with black and white and brown. Then we cut to a group in blues and greens, then yellow and orange; and finally, first to dull, then to flaming reds. The lighting as well as the costumes contrives to accentuate the mounting drama of the scene. Change of light is justified by the blowing out of the candles, and the lighting then moves from white to straw colour, to amber and then to red over the entire action.

This Waterloo sequence, of course, is the dramatic highlight of the film, the only time when world-shattering events impinge on the private comedy of manners. Elsewhere, colour is used less ostentatiously but equally theatrically. Theatrical, in fact, is the key word for *Becky Sharp*, which has solved the tricky problem of reducing Thackeray's sprawling novel, *Vanity Fair*, to manageable proportions – without losing its bite – by placing it under the sign of the theatre. The very first shot is of rich blue curtains, parting as a head pops through and the pupils of Miss Pinkerton's Academy gather to witness the departure of Becky and Amelia – the latter to her wealthy family, the former to a cold, friendless world. The girls flutter like bright, delicately plumaged birds round the formidable Miss Pinkerton, stiff and black in her severe pince-nez and lace, as Becky, cued by the arrival of the eligible and obviously susceptible Joseph Sedley, Amelia's brother, delivers her first aria: 'I have no destination. Not until I have found a room, a garret, a pillow to lay my head on.'

In the novel, Becky already has an invitation to stay with the Sedleys when the action starts; in the film she wangles one through her touching pose as a homeless waif. The film thus not only short-circuits several chapters of the

Becky Sharp: Becky performs for Miss Julia (Alison Skipworth) and on stage at Bath

book, but brings its unwieldy wealth of characters under control by instantly pinpointing Becky as the puppet-master who will pull their strings. Surrounded by specific theatrical references – her mother's career as a dancer, the trunk full of costumes and properties she carries about with her, her stage appearance in Bath after her downfall in 'Selected Songs by Mme Rebecque' – Becky makes of herself her greatest creation, even her own emotions being subject to the ambiguous demands of her *mise en scène*. There is a fine moment of pure theatre at the end of the Waterloo sequence when everyone has gone, leaving Becky alone on the ballroom stairs. Her husband Rawdon enters to say goodbye before rejoining his regiment: 'I've drunk, I've gambled, but I've always loved you.' Touched, and with complete sincerity, Becky cries 'I want you back!' and sinks down on the stairs in despair as he leaves. A moment later she is selling a pair of horses to Joseph Sedley at an exorbitant price; she looks down from the balcony at the departing soldiers with tender concern, crying, 'The marching men … in an hour they'll be dying for their country'; and she turns back with a shrug, 'Well, I'm dying for my breakfast.'

So far Becky has been doing the string-pulling; but in her dealings with the Marquis of Steyne, she at last seems to be trapped by a greater puppet-master into revealing her true feelings. The stage is exquisitely set. In a garden bower, Becky sits prettily singing, twirling flowers in her hands as the Marquis offers to lend her the money Rawdon needs, provided she grants him 'the little supper' for which he has waited so patiently. Gracefully she offers him a flower. 'Thank you, my dear,' he says, 'and now go on with your singing'; she complies, and the camera comes to rest on her lap as, one by one, banknotes shower down to settle there. Cut to Becky giving Rawdon the money, urging him to go and pay his debt at once; then a slow track in to a gauze curtain behind which Becky is entertaining the Marquis to his intimate supper, sweetly coaxing that there is some good in every wolf in an attempt to get out of her part of the bargain, but finding that she has met her match. 'Poor, optimistic lamb,' he snarls. Enter the furious Rawdon. 'Why squabble over something you don't own and I don't want?' asks the Marquis; and Becky, abandoned by both men, is left weeping on the floor, crying 'My love for you is the only real thing in my life. Don't take it away from me,' as Rawdon leaves. But even before Becky lifts her head to add, 'They'll all laugh at me. Oh, how they'll all laugh', the game is given away by the exquisite Aubusson carpet on which she has chosen to fall – a prima donna arranging her big scene, ready for the curtain call.

Throughout, the colour underlines this propensity of Becky's to dramatise in her careful choice of costume. Soft blues for melting ingenuousness, bright yellow for moments of triumph; bold check for her brightening entry into Sir Pitt Crawley's dun-coloured home, white for the tragedy of love betrayed on the Aubusson carpet; deceptively demure pink for her stage appearance as a shepherdess singing 'The Lass with the Delicate Air' which ends with her furiously throwing her basket of flowers at the jeering audience. And the neatest touch of all, flamboyant tartan with an insolently nodding green feather – green 'for safety and hope' – as we last see her hurling a book of good works at the priggish Pitt Crawley and preparing to set off in search of new worlds to conquer.

In many ways *Becky Sharp* is not only excellent Thackeray but perfect Mamoulian. Picking up Becky in the opening scene and gauging her instantly,

Becky Sharp: '… And now go on with your singing.' Cedric Hardwicke and Miriam Hopkins

his camera seems to dart with her through her picaresque adventures without pause. Partly because his camera, as always, seems one step ahead of his characters, planning and executing the move into the next scene almost before they have got there; and partly because the novel has been so intelligently pared that each sequence seems to have its unnecessary beginning and end cut off, as in Godard's *À bout de souffle*. Nothing is explained, everything has to be picked up on the wing. At Miss Pinkerton's, for instance, Becky has set her cap, along with her plea for 'a room, a garret, a pillow', at fat but wealthy Joseph Sedley. A moment later at the Sedleys', George is proposing to Amelia, Joseph almost but not quite to Becky, and she is off as governess to Sir Pitt Crawley's horrible family. One look at his handsome son Rawdon, and she is off where the money lies, as companion to Rawdon's rich and doting Aunt Julia. Instantly Aunt Julia is looking into the tinselly secrets of Becky's trunk, and

Becky Sharp: 'Oh, how they'll all laugh …' Mamoulian on set with Miriam Hopkins

Becky, after shedding copious yarns and crocodile tears, is off to Brighton, married to Rawdon.

There, in a brilliant scene occasioned by the poverty of both runaway couples, Mamoulian draws a watershed between sharp Becky and sweet Amelia. A sheet divides the room. On one side, Amelia demurely pours the tea. On the other, Becky flirts with Amelia's George until Rawdon enters, when she joins Amelia, and both girls are seen in silhouette through the sheet. As they sit chastely side by side playing the spinet, news arrives that Napoleon has escaped from Elba and war is imminent. 'How terrible,' says Amelia. 'How amusing,' says Becky. Later, in one of the film's most brilliant ellipses, we have just learned of George Osborne's death in battle from a terse scene where Amelia kneels beside a plaque with his name on it, when a dissolve takes us from her grief-stricken face to a glittering banquet presided over by Becky, seated next to the Marquis and shortly to be presented (another superbly terse, *tableau vivant* scene) to the Prince Regent.

With the novel thus stripped down to its narrative drive with almost comic strip simplicity – though retaining Becky's complex character – it was

Becky Sharp: Sir Pitt Crawley (George Hassell) with his new governess

obviously essential that each moment, more particularly each character, should make their mark instantly. And here the film is triumphantly successful, surpassing even George Cukor's *David Copperfield* in the truculent self-confidence of its casting. Miriam Hopkins's Becky – it almost goes without saying, in that the film practically stands or falls by her rightness – is superb, Thackeray's artful, enchanting vixen to the life, 'small and slight in person; pale, sandy-haired, and with eyes habitually cast down: when they looked up they were very large, odd and attractive; so attractive that the Reverend Mr Crisp, fresh from Oxford ... fell in love with Miss Sharp; being shot dead by a glance of her eyes which was fired all the way across Chiswick Church from the school-pew to the reading desk'. But supporting her is a gallery of minor characters straight from Thackeray's pages, so self-contained in their roles in the story that no elaboration is necessary: Alan Mowbray as the large, handsome, stupid Rawdon; Cedric Hardwicke as the vulpine Marquis; Nigel Bruce as the bovine Joseph; Frances Dee as sweet, silly, weepy Amelia; Alison Skipworth as the tartly good-natured, wealthily eccentric Miss Julia; and so on right down the line to the insect-like Miss Pinkerton (Elspeth Dudgeon) and the creakingly elegant Prince Regent (Olaf Hytten) – all instantly recognisable as the posturing caricatures who inhabit Vanity Fair.

So, according to the history books, ended Mamoulian's creative career.

On 10 October of that year, 1935, his remarkable production of *Porgy and Bess* opened at the Alvin Theatre, New York.

9: *The Gay Desperado*

For his next film, Jesse Lasky proposed an adaptation of *Faust*. Instead, Mamoulian chose an operetta about a comic Mexican bandit who is inspired to reorganise his outlaw band as a Chicago mob after seeing an American gangster movie, meanwhile abducting a young tenor to satisfy his craving for music, and benevolently fostering a romance between the singer and a girl who has become the mob's first, not unwilling, kidnap victim. Not, on the face of it, particularly promising material; but had the songs been written by Rodgers and Hart, and had the singing hero (Nino Martini) been as adept at self-parody as Jeanette MacDonald, *The Gay Desperado* might have outdone even *Love Me Tonight*. As it is, it can still give a head start to any other 1930s musical and win hands down (operatic arias notwithstanding) in charm and eccentricity.

In the first place, Mamoulian obviously fell for the picturesque vistas offered by colonial architecture, haciendas, cactuses and sombreros, and the exteriors are a series of magnificent images, beautifully shot by Lucien Andriot in rich textures of sunlight and shadow which make one almost swear after the film is over that it was in colour, or at least tinted. Great sweeping panoramas pick up the bandits as they billow in clouds of dust past graceful archways, curving walls and pale, crenellated churches. Dark silhouettes ride out against the desert skyline, or pick their way through jagged rows of giant cactus. Towering shadows flicker over the obligingly white walls as the outlaws crouch round the campfire in the moonlight, line up in the sun to form a firing-squad, or simply stand at ease with their ponchos and sombreros making their own pleasing echoes.

In the second place, he bolsters a tolerably witty script, making it seem much funnier than it is, by his prolific invention. The basic joke is the incongruity of moustachioed Mexicans trying to behave like underworld hoods and getting hopelessly tangled in the jargon, sometimes with almost surrealist thoroughness. Dictating a ransom note, for instance, the bandit chief (Leo Carrillo) cheerfully begins, 'Señor Shay, hello!' only to be pulled up by his sneering lieutenant: 'That's wrong. Hello is telephone. You should say Dear Gentleman.' Later, the same lieutenant indignantly reprimands a firing-squad victim for refusing, on the grounds that he doesn't smoke, the traditional courtesy cigarette: 'You've got the worstest manners of any hombre I ever killed.' Normally, such humour soon palls, however well done, but not with Mamoulian ringing the changes in a welter of gags, in-jokes and bizarre characterisations.

The Gay Desperado

Cheerfully cannibalising himself, he turns the final sequence into a send-up of *City Streets*, with the mob taking the lovers for a ride in order to unite rather than part them. The arrival of real American gangsters in Mexico on a takeover bid for the new mob is the signal for a series of neat parodies: a slick-haired, coin-flipping George Raft, a cigar-chewing Edward G. Robinson, a sneering, snarling Cagney. Harold Huber, playing Leo Carrillo's sinister and bloodthirsty lieutenant – black-garbed and black-avised in a prophetic caricature of Humphrey Bogart's villain in *The Oklahoma Kid* – suddenly launches into a wistful defence of his pet 'Mickey the Mice' after denouncing nasty gangster movies. And Mischa Auer has a splendid running gag all to himself whereby he sits brooding throughout, disapprovingly silent in the traditional pose of the peon, until finally, driven beyond all forbearance by the goings on, he explodes into a magnificent plea on behalf of the national bandit industry.

The Gay Desperado: Nino Martini faces the firing squad

The story, even in comic opera terms, scarcely bears examination, but Mamoulian allows none. From the opening shots of a gunfight in the streets and a body being thrown out of a car as someone cheerfully bellows 'Give 'em the woiks!' – dissolving back to show enthralled Mexicans watching a film – he keeps the action whisking along so airily that its feet barely touch the ground. The fight in the cinema started by irritated patrons when Carrillo interrupts the screening to announce his inspiration, quickly quelled by the singer with the golden voice; the kidnapping of the singer; the takeover of the radio station to let him fulfil his heart's desire of broadcasting (very funny, this, with three Mexican Andrews Sisters idiotically continuing to sing 'Lookee, lookee, lookee!' after the hold-up, holding their hands up as requested but still managing to wave them rhythmically); and then his training as a bandit, culminating in his encounter with the love of his life when, out on his first job, he embarks on a hold-up with a diffident 'Stop the car, please', eliciting from the victim (a spirited Ida Lupino) a disparaging 'Something told me this was amateur night.'

Linking it all is a splendidly funny performance by Leo Carrillo – 'the worst bad man in this whole country' – alternating hypothetical cruelties with tearful sentimentalities, the latter generally occasioned by music and evoking fond memories of one of his eleven wives (usually the wrong one, as his lieutenant never tires of pointing out). Carrillo repeated this comic Spaniard performance virtually unchanged throughout his career, but never so enter-tainingly as here, where every imaginable cliché is taken to extremes and given new, mocking life. Even the obligatory fight between bandit hero and captive heroine, when he tries to break down her resistance by saying that she really loves him in spite of everything, takes an agreeable twist when, after a battle worthy of a pair of John Ford Irishmen, he sadly sues for peace: 'I have made a great mistake. It is not you who love me. It is I who love you.'

Even Mamoulian, however, can do very little about the songs, which are in the popular-operatic vein, laboriously dropped into the action with the camera condemned to stand more or less still while Nino Martini moons solemnly through 'O Celeste Aida', 'Mamacita Mia', or 'The World is Mine Tonight'. There is one nicely malevolent shot of Mischa Auer screwing up his face in agony and disappearing beneath his sombrero as Martini grabs the

microphone in the radio station; and another delightful piece of business when a police officer, handcuffed to the singing bandit, already carried away by the aria, suddenly realises to his embarrassment that his arm is involuntarily echoing the tenor's expansive gestures. But with the time-honoured routine – tender pose; 'I can't talk, but I can sing it'; deep breath – with which the romantic 'The World is Mine Tonight' is introduced, we are a long way from the serpentine subtleties of 'Isn't It Romantic?'

The Gay Desperado: Ida Lupino, Nino Martini and James Blakeley

10: *High, Wide and Handsome*

The Gay Desperado, engaging and easy on the eye as it is, is of no great consequence. *High, Wide and Handsome*, on the other hand, is the most persistently underrated of all Mamoulian's films: a sort of musical Western which anticipates the serene and summery blend of fairytale, fact and fantasy of such post-war Renoir films as *French Cancan* and *Eléna et les hommes*.

The story, an original by Oscar Hammerstein II, concerns the true history of the discovery of the Pennsylvania oilfields in 1859, and the epic struggle waged by the poor farmer-prospectors against the railroad freight tycoons who resorted to every means in their power, financial and physical, to prevent the completion of the pipelines which would bring oil to every home in America. Hammerstein, it seems, wrote a gay and fluffy musical comedy; Mamoulian rewrote it with him, putting its feet back on the ground with a good deal of accurate background detail. The result, as Richard Roud has said (National Film Theatre programme note), is 'an extraordinary fusion of Brecht and Broadway'.

Not that *High, Wide and Handsome* is particularly didactic in intent, but it does very effectively follow Brecht's principle outlined in the *Little Organum for the Theatre*: 'As we cannot invite the public to fling itself into the story as if it were a river, and let itself be swept vaguely to and fro, the individual events have to be knotted together in such a way that the knots are easily seen. The events must not succeed one another indistinguishably but must give us a chance to interpose our judgment.' On the one hand, there is the basically realistic treatment of the historical facts: the prospectors toiling to build the pipelines clear across the state through snow and forest and over mountains to the

High, Wide and Handsome: the medicine show and the moonlit orchard. Irene Dunne with Raymond Walburn (top) and Randolph Scott

refineries; the chicanery of rising freight prices countered by farmers contributing their life savings; the gangs of mercenaries sent out to terrorise the builders and destroy their work. On the other, the rustic never-never village of Titusville, with its rose-covered cottages and dainty farmyards where hero and heroine conduct their idyllic romance. Knotting the two together, such splendid alienation effects as the pastoral wedding in which the guests, parading in their gingham and frockcoat finery, are showered by sprays of gushing oil, or the magnificent ride to the rescue of an entire circus troupe just as the heroes, within sight of success as they hoist the last pipes up a sheer mountain rock-face, are attacked by the villains brandishing whips and pickaxes.

Brecht's alienation or *Verfremdungseffekt*, as John Willett defines it (*The Theatre of Bertolt Brecht*), is 'a matter of detachment, of reorientation: exactly what Shelley meant when he wrote that poetry "makes familiar objects to be as if they were not familiar" or Schopenhauer when he claimed that art must show "common objects of experience in a light that is at once clear and unfamiliar"'. This, in a light-hearted way, is precisely what Mamoulian does in *High, Wide and Handsome*, starting with the opening shot, a close-up of Irene Dunne on a stage singing the title song: slowly the camera tracks back to reveal, not a theatre, but a caravan in the middle of a town square where the proprietor of a medicine show is preparing to hawk his elixir of life, 'Indian Wizard Oil'.

The caravan catches fire, and the homeless Irene Dunne is put up for the night by a handsome young farmer (Randolph Scott) and his archetypal grandmother, all grumbles and goodheartedness (Elizabeth Patterson). Next morning Irene Dunne gazes rapturously round the shining little farmhouse with the hoard of heirloom treasures, portraits and knick-knacks watched over by the family Bible: 'It's like a picture-book,' she cries. 'A farm's hard work,' replies Elizabeth Patterson tartly, and Mamoulian obliges with a charming confirmation of both points of view when Irene Dunne trips out to the muddy yard to feed the animals with a blithe 'Hello, chickens!', terrifying the life out of both them and herself; and then, getting the hang of it and singing gaily, is rewarded by snorts from the pigs and by a chorus line of horses listening approvingly. The young couple, inevitably, are instantly attracted to each other, and romance flourishes in the ethereally balmy setting of a moonlit orchard where he gently showers her with apple blossoms as she holds her face up to the moon 'like I was drowning in silver'. As in the scene between the little dancer and her prince on the rosily moonlit Butte de Montmartre in *French Cancan*, the setting is impossibly artificial; and yet, partly because of this, it becomes a moment lifted out of time and space into the secure, enchanted world of dreams.

At the other end of the scale to this fairy-tale world, lies the gritty reality of the oil business, with its huge derricks mushrooming up and threatening to swamp the tranquil little town, and the superb panoramas worthy of John Ford over snowy landscapes, hills and black pine forests as the epic task of laying the pipelines gets under way and tired men sit through the night, rifles across their knees, to guard their handiwork. Both elements, of course, are 'common objects of experience', the staple diet of Hollywood romance and Hollywood adventure. Yet in juxtaposition, each somehow takes on a new reality, given a touch of Schopenhauer's 'clear and unfamiliar light'; and one becomes involved in the struggles of the farmers, or the despair of Irene Dunne when her husband neglects her in order to conduct the war, to an extent that is not warranted by the events themselves. And chief among the 'easily seen' Brechtian knots are the tolerably absurd machinations of the bad men.

Like Renoir's villains, Walt Brennan (Alan Hale) and Joe Varese (Akim Tamiroff) 'have their reasons', are rather likeable, and are not taken too seriously. Brennan, the railroad tycoon with the bluff smile and a girl on each knee, is mainly concerned with defending his creature comforts, and when defeat comes he simply bows to the inevitable, making an undignified exit by putting on the top hat which someone has filled with oil. Varese, the dandified and decadent proprietor of the Hunky Dory Saloon who finds himself in a handsome position for blackmail, endearingly excuses his wicked ways (he forces Scott to sell a piece of land on which his wife has set her heart for a dream house) by referring to his own dear but departed wife, seen in a photograph as a vampiric creature clutching a rose between her gnashing teeth. Yet it is Brennan who incites the violence which explodes in the final fight; and Varese who, to satisfy a whim, is directly responsible for breaking up the young couple's marriage.

To analyse the film in these terms, of course, is to be hopelessly ponderous about it – Mamoulian was not trying to make a Brechtian analysis of the human condition along the lines of *The Caucasian Chalk Circle* or *The Good*

Woman of Setzuan – and I have done so simply because the attitude is so widespread that in *High, Wide and Handsome* he wrecked a good historical Western by getting frivolous about it, or alternatively, wrecked a good musical by getting too serious about it. The truth is that he has simply instilled a little reality and a little human feeling into the artificial world of the musical. There is a charmingly tender scene, for instance, when Randolph Scott steals home late one night to his wife, guiltily aware that he has been neglecting her because crisis after crisis in the oil business has taken up so much of his time, and she wakens to find him standing beside her bed, showering her with apple blossoms in an apologetic romantic reminiscence. She is delighted, until a message arrives to summon him to an urgent meeting, when she angrily hurls his olive branch away. In the following scene, to avert the new crisis, the farmers assert their faith in him by drawing out their life savings to give him the support he needs. Two kinds of love, both conventional, yet gently querying their conventions by their juxtaposition.

High, Wide and Handsome: Joe Varese (Akim Tamiroff) in his sanctum

Similarly, it is no accident that, dropped into the middle of the sub-plot featuring Dorothy Lamour as the usual no-better-than-she-ought-to-be entertainer, there is a scene which might well be a fugitive from Fritz Lang's *Fury*. Hurt and bleeding, she is hounded like an animal through the black, storm-ridden night by a mob headed by a hell-fire preacher screaming 'Make that Jezebel walk, drag her by the hair', till she falls exhausted at Irene Dunne's sheltering feet. The friendship between the two girls is casually established in two delightful sequences where Irene Dunne tries (without success) to teach her friend, a sophisticated nightclub chanteuse, how to belt out the beer-hall songs which will enable her to make a humbler but more honest living. Later, when Dorothy Lamour has backslid into becoming the tycoon's pampered mistress, her obligatory change of heart – when she comes to the aid of the good guys – is given just that touch of genuine feeling which will lift it out of the rut by the memory of these scenes.

Even in his manipulation of the settings, Mamoulian maintains this tension between real and unreal, contrasting not only the natural locations with the studio sets, but two kinds of dream world (the luminous paradise of the village, and the tawdry glitter of the medicine shows and the circus) and two kinds of reality (the rolling hills of snow and pines, and the man-made dirt and derricks of the oilfields). And bridging the rival worlds, some marvellously ambivalent detail: the little back room reached by way of the beer and sawdust of the saloon, an Aladdin's cave of plush and gilt fineries where Joe Varese transacts his business festooned in cats, parrots and gilded cages; the dance in the village barn attended by mare and foal in their stall and solemnly watched from the rafters by a grave old owl; the showdown fight with its bizarre spectacle of elephants trumpeting to the rescue, while bearded lady, strongman and dwarfs lay about them with a will and acrobats shin up the cliff-face to carry on the good work of getting the pipes to the top.

At heart, of course, *High, Wide and Handsome* is first and foremost a musical, and one which breaks all records for attack by having Irene Dunne, in close-up, belt into the title number from the first foot of the first shot. Significantly, perhaps, Mamoulian's camera seems here to have found a new, majestic freedom in the epic sweep of the action scenes, the breathtaking

(next page) High, Wide and Handsome: the circus to the rescue

overhead set-ups for the circus rescue, the superb crane shot down from the banked candles in the circus big top to a close shot of Irene Dunne as she starts to sing 'Can I Forget You?' And although most of the half-dozen charming songs contributed by Kern and Hammerstein are handled more or less straight – the mournful torch song, 'The Things I Want', sung in a nightclub by Dorothy Lamour; 'Can I Forget You?' sung by Irene Dunne in the moonlit orchard and grandly reprised in the middle of a circus ring; the catchy, bouncy 'Allegheny Al', sung on a saloon table-top by both girls – one sequence takes an entirely different turn.

Irene Dunne and Randolph Scott have just been married, and the celebrations start with one of the guests (William Frawley) singing the ebullient 'Will You Marry Me Tomorrow, Maria?' Suddenly he jumps down from the bandstand, sweeping the guests across the lawn and into the song, and the dance begins. The young couple steal away to the idyllic little clearing on

High, Wide and Handsome: 'Can I Forget You …': Irene Dunne in the circus big top

the hilltop where they plan to build their house and where she sings 'The Folks Who Live on the Hill'. Cut back to the dance as they rejoin it, and just as a loud explosion is followed by great sprays of oil gushing over the lawn. In both its rhythms and general layout – men grouped by the beer barrels, ladies by the tea tables – the sequence clearly foreshadows the 'Independence Day' picnic in *Summer Holiday*; but it is also the first significant appearance of dance in Mamoulian's films (not merely dancing in itself, but choreography simulated by camera movement), and as such it points clearly forward to the all-singing, all-dancing splendours that were to come in *Summer Holiday* and *Silk Stockings*.

11: *Golden Boy*

After *High, Wide and Handsome* Mamoulian took a curiously retrogressive step in directing *Golden Boy*: his own choice, as a second-best when Harry Cohn of Columbia refused to consider a film of *Porgy and Bess*. Even in 1939, two years after the Group Theatre premiere, Clifford Odets's play must have been looking a little naïve, if not quite so shopworn as it does today with its pseudo-popular idiom, its sentimentalised 'we are the little people' characters, and its 'workers of the world' philosophy.

Mamoulian wanted Odets to adapt his own work, but – perhaps fortunately – Odets was not available and instead he found two fledgling writers, Daniel Taradash and Lewis Meltzer, and between them they stripped the play down to produce a workable script. The character of Frank, the Labour Organiser, has gone altogether, and with him most of the dubious philosophising which makes young Joe Bonaparte's choice – between being a sensitive, long-haired, penniless violinist and a tough, brutalised, well-paid boxer – a matter for social concern in terms of the struggle between Capital and Labour. Instead the film makes the decision largely a moral and personal one, with its real climax the murderous championship fight rather than Joe's *crise de conscience*.

Also carefully pruned are most of the poetic excesses. For instance, the solemn incantation by Joe's girl, Lorna, at the end of the play, after he has killed his opponent in the fight: 'Somewhere there must be happy boys and girls who can teach us the way of life. We'll find some city where poverty's no shame – where music is no crime – where there's no war in the streets – where a man is glad to be himself, to live and make his woman herself.' Somehow, one cannot

imagine these words passing the lips of tough, wisecracking Barbara Stanwyck, who plays the role in the film. Instead of the soppy, slightly tarnished girl of the original, we get a hard-boiled, embittered woman who succumbs to a streak of romantic tenderness in falling for the golden boy; and at the end her speech is much simpler and much more true: 'Be glad you're rid of him, you're free … Now you can go back to yourself, to your music … Nothing can stop you when you do what's in your heart.'

This toughening, lightening process is further advanced by the brilliant casting and performances of Adolphe Menjou as Joe's fight manager, and Joseph Calleia as the trigger-happy gangster who insists on 'buying a piece of him'. Menjou, trailing his usual aura of world-weary sophistication, brings a touch of elegant despair to his love for Lorna which reflects some of its own genuineness on to her affair with Joe; while Calleia, an exact caricature of Bogart in pinstripe suit, carnation and snap-brim hat, snarling his lines with

Golden Boy: Barbara Stanwyk, Sam Levene, Jospeh Calleia, Adolphe Menjou and Edward S. Brophy

hand firmly rammed in suspiciously bulging pocket, inhabits that unsettling serio-comic ground between laughter and menace. Even more importantly, the expansive playing of Menjou and Calleia tends to take the centre of the stage, at least slightly dimming the tearful excesses of Joe's father, with his hangdog moustache, tiresome Italianisms ('Take-a-dis violin …') and heartfelt cries of 'Money, money! We got *souls*. We got to take care of 'em!'

These excesses still remain, of course, and Mamoulian does his best to make them acceptable through the loving care with which he presents the Bonaparte home, a monument to lower-middle-class comfort, every monstrous detail of which can be seen and studied as the family poses in a pensive group while Joe plays his violin: floral wallpaper and swathing curtains, fringed lampshades and antimacassars, Victorian bric-à-brac crammed into every conceivable corner and on to every surface. But the tone is set,

Golden Boy: William H. Strauss, Lee J. Cobb, Sam Levene, Barbara Stanwyk, Beatrice Blinn and William Holden

appropriately enough, by Joseph Calleia's refugee from *Scarface*, with the result that *Golden Boy* looks as though it had been made seven or eight years earlier at the time of the first gangster movies: a sister piece, in fact, to *City Streets*.

Even for Mamoulian the opening sequences are exceptionally bold and swift. A shot of a New York street; a quick dissolve to a closer shot; closer yet, a window from the outside; from the inside, Menjou on the phone discussing divorce with his wife and marriage, in whiplash dialogue, with Stanwyck: 'Then we can get married. Otherwise I'm just a dame from Newark' – 'I've been off the gold standard for ages. I'm down for the count.' Joe (William Holden) bursts in, starts talking at once, and badgers Menjou into the lift and all the way down the street in an attempt to persuade him that he could be a future champion. The whole sequence reproduces exactly the fast, wisecracking

Golden Boy: Menjou and Stanwyk

brashness typical of the early 1930s, and the period feeling increases as the film continues. Echoes of both *Applause* and *City Streets* abound: Joe and his father talking at night in the back yard, illuminated by flickering neon signs against a city skyline; a love scene between Joe and Lorna on top of a skyscraper, and another in which they gaze at Brooklyn Bridge in the moonlight; the same sense of stylised doom (the lovers) and menace (the gangsters) as for the Cooper-Sidney couple. Above all there is the same expressionist touch in the angles, shadows and lighting contrasts.

Memorable chiefly as an *exercice de style*, *Golden Boy* is also distinguished by its excellent performances – in addition to Calleia, Menjou and Stanwyck, William Holden is good, unshowy and sincere in the title role, his film début – and by the climactic fight scene. Shot unsparingly as a long, brutish slugging match, interspersed with pitilessly accurate shots of the excited, exultant crowd screaming for more blood, it takes the film on to an altogether different plane from Odets's naïvely idealistic morality play about the clash between art and money. A double-pronged attack, alas, is busily at work pulling it down again. 'Miss Moon, you sweet, gentle, good,' Joe's father has already told Lorna, 'You friend of my son. He's gotta big trouble in his heart.' When Joe meets a quavery old Negro after the fight, father of the boxer he killed, who echoes old Bonaparte's sentiments – 'We just little people, and all of us got a burden, even you' – it is just too much.

12: *The Mark of Zorro*

Moving over to 20th Century-Fox for the first of three films he made there, Mamoulian filled a curious gap in his eclectic choice of subjects: despite his gift for movement and his brilliant visual flair, he had not yet tackled a real action picture, a cloak-and-sword swashbuckler. *The Mark of Zorro* rectified the omission so well that it is one of the masterpieces of the genre, while at the same time escaping from it.

Many critics, then and later, sighed nostalgically for the good old days of Fred Niblo's silent version, which was a whirlwind of stunts and chases in which the dashing Douglas Fairbanks, sword and teeth flashing with equal brilliance, popped up triumphantly everywhere at once behind the Zorro mask. Tyrone Power, they said, was tame stuff by comparison, unable to match the spring-heeled Fairbanks athletics; but what they failed to notice was that he didn't need to, since Mamoulian was doing the swashbuckling for him.

One of the most striking action sequences in the film is Zorro's arrival in the palace to terrorise the corrupt Governor, and his subsequent escape pursued by Captain Pasquale's men. The sequence begins with a shot of the Governor (J. Edward Bromberg) sitting writing at his desk. The camera pans gently right, and a rapier-point flicks into frame to snuff out the candle. The Governor looks round, mystified; Zorro emerges from hiding, delivers his message of warning, carves his Z on the wall ('This will remind you that I have been here once and can return'), and vanishes the way he came. Pasquale, entering to find the petrified Governor blindfolded and pinned down by a sword propped against his throat, furiously turns out the guard. Cut to the garden, a flurry of torches, guards running to and fro; Zorro, in a monk's habit, sidles into the chapel where

he encounters the Governor's niece Lolita (Linda Darnell) at her prayers, and in a charmingly funny scene gets tangled up in his disguises as she soulfully inquires if it's a sin to want to marry rather than enter a convent, while he tries to catch a glimpse of her modestly veiled face. Suddenly she notices a sword protruding beneath his habit; thrilled, she does not give him away when guards enter to search the chapel. A lovely shot of Lolita sweeping through the garden, another of the monk downing a guard, leaping into a bush, and re-emerging a moment later in Zorro's black. Then a fine flurry of action in which he escapes up a tree, over the wall, through the wood to his horse, and gallops away with the soldiers in hopeless pursuit.

The first thing one notices about this sequence is how little (with the exception of the romantic interlude in the chapel) Zorro actually does, his menace being suggested by a sword point, his actions by sudden camera movements in the semi-obscurity of the garden. The second thing is that, although the whole sequence gives the impression of being one continuous movement, it is in fact – even the final flight over the wall – composed of a series of brief shots. Here Mamoulian is able to make full and free use of his

The Mark of Zorro: Tyrone Power, J. Edward Bromberg and Gale Sondergaard

technique of cutting on movement without interrupting the flow of an action, and which he was soon to apply so successfully to the dance routines in *Summer Holiday* and *Silk Stockings*.

Apart from the obligatory scenes of his duel with Pasquale and the final showdown, Zorro is in fact seen in action remarkably infrequently: once he robs the Governor as he flees the country in his coach, and twice he summarily relieves the tax-collectors of money they have taken from the poor, and that is all. It is no accident that our first glimpse of him as young Don Diego, pride of the military academy in Madrid, is at a graduation ceremony where half a dozen exquisitely matched shots equate his horsemanship with the grace and skill of a dancer. After the demonstration, talking to his friends, he announces his intention of returning to peaceful California, where there are no longer even Indians to fight. 'What will you do with your sword, then?' someone asks. 'This!' he replies, tossing it point first to the roof, where it hangs quivering. (The same gesture ends the film.) Aesthete and romantic, Diego intends to devote himself to living and loving, and even his enforced masquerade as Zorro does not suffice to turn him from his purpose.

As soon as he reaches Los Angeles (the Spanish city of 1820), he learns that his father has been deposed as Alcalde, and that the country is in the grip of tyranny and corruption. Yet his first appearance is not as Zorro, but as the effete dandy he uses to cloak his activities. 'Swordplay is such a *violent* business,' he sighs, dabbing his mouth daintily with a lace handkerchief as Captain Pasquale (Basil Rathbone) strides in, rapier in hand, on his first courtesy visit to the new Governor. And almost immediately he catches his first glimpse of Lolita through the window, a vision of radiant beauty in white, a white cat on her knee as she sits wreathed in blossoms under a tree in the garden. From that moment on, Zorro's mission as an avenger comes second to his purpose as a lover.

Apart from the scene in the chapel, there is a beautiful two-part sequence starting with the dinner on the terrace of the Governor's house at which Diego is to be introduced to Lolita. Much to his delight, a marriage of convenience has been arranged; much to her distress, since she is already half in love with the mysterious Zorro, he makes a superbly laconic entry to the moonlit patio under the trees where soft shadows play romantically and an orchestra is tucked discreetly away in the gloom. 'You'll forgive me for being late, señor,' he says

apologetically. 'They heated the water for my bath too early.' Diego and Lolita dance under the trees charmingly. 'I never dreamed dancing could be so wonderful,' she sighs. 'I found it rather fatiguing,' he replies crushingly. She rushes out in distress, and Diego asks for her hand in marriage, adding, with devastating offhandedness as he takes a pinch of snuff, 'A refusal would crush me.' Cut. A rose thrown in at Lolita's window falls on her dress as she sits at her dressing table, and Zorro appears on her balcony like Romeo, inadvertently revealing his true identity. 'Perhaps,' says Lolita sweetly, 'I could learn to tolerate Diego. I do so want to please Uncle Luis.'

With Diego so relaxed and so busy pursuing romance, the active role is taken over, paradoxically, by the evil Captain Pasquale, pleasingly portrayed by Basil Rathbone as a sort of neurotic jack-in-the-box. 'He's always stabbing at something,' complains the Governor as Pasquale, irritated by Lolita's defence of Zorro at the dinner table, furiously spears an orange; and one suddenly realises that each time one has seen him, he has either been making a practice

The Mark of Zorro: the dinner on the terrace; the final duel. Rathbone and Power

lunge with his rapier or preparing to do so, and seems unable to function properly, seems undressed even, without a sword in his hand. One of the most galvanic moments in the film is the electrifyingly abrupt and athletic knee-bend with which he limbers up before his duel with Zorro, flicking his rapier out with lightning ease to lop the top off one of the candles on the desk. 'Ha! Ha!' he cries contemptuously as Zorro repeats the gesture and the candle continues to burn; then Zorro smilingly lifts off the top to show that it is cut in two. The duel that follows is superb, all the more savage for its brevity, ending with Pasquale pierced through the heart and falling back against the wall to dislodge a picture which conceals Zorro's mark: '... I have been here once and can return.'

Also paradoxically, it is not – unlike every other version of the story – Zorro's black mask which is the dominant motif of the film, but Pasquale's dazzling white breeches, somehow at odds with the mellow, whitewashed stones of the Spanish houses and churches. Which is, after all, as it should be, since this is Diego's rightful home and Pasquale is the usurper. In a sense,

Pasquale is an anachronism. As Diego jokingly says in his dandy role: 'Dashing about with a cutlass is quite out of fashion; hasn't been done since the Middle Ages.' And Pasquale's death, taking with him the omnipresent image of his drawn rapier, sets a curiously final seal on the restoration of peace and order of the end, when Diego can once again throw his rapier to the roof and devote his life and his love to Lolita.

The Mark of Zorro may be 'only' a swashbuckler, but it is one of Mamoulian's most elegant and intelligent films.

13: *Blood and Sand*

The six years since *Becky Sharp* had seen considerable improvements in the Technicolor process, and Mamoulian's second encounter with colour was almost as fruitful as his first. With its elegantly swirling capes and statuesque groupings, its rich romantic aura of love in the moonlight and death in the afternoon, and its superb colour effects setting the dusty ochres of the arena scenes against the glowing blues and crimsons of the costumes and interiors, *Blood and Sand* all but brings off the tricky task of dominating the melodrama inherent in Ibañez's story of a matador's progress from rags to riches and retribution. Only at the end does the plot begin to pile up and get out of hand.

In an interesting article in *American Cinematographer* (June 1941) Mamoulian has described how many sequences in the film were deliberately styled after certain painters. For instance, Murillo bronzes, browns and blacks for Juan's poverty-stricken childhood; Goya, of course, for the bullring; Velazquez for Doña Sol's mansion (in essential flavour rather than detail: Velazquez as the master of light and shadow, of the richness of court life); El Greco for the matador's chapel; fourteenth-century primitives for the death of Nacional (because he is a primitive); sixteenth-century Venetians for Juan's dressing room, with the luxurious colour and bustling movement of Titian and Veronese in the ceremonial robing of Juan; Sorolla for the street and market scenes; and so on.

To anyone not particularly well versed in the history of art, most of these derivations will probably pass unnoticed; but not the reasons, emotional and visual, for their adoption. After the long childhood sequence, dominated by the drab browns and blacks of poverty, the first splash of colour comes with the

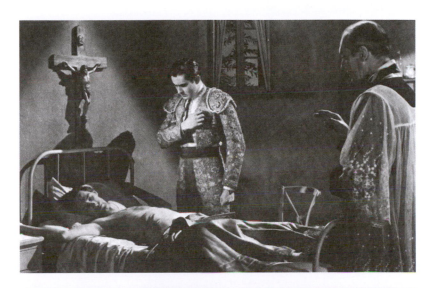

Blood and Sand: the death of the Nacional and the return from Madrid. Tyrone Power with John Carradine (above) and Anthony Quinn

shock of a window opening on a new world. Juan and his boyhood friends, having run away to Madrid to learn the art of the ring, are returning ten years later as fully fledged bullfighters. On the train taking them home they talk, and someone addresses a question to Juan, lying stretched out on the seat. He lowers his newspaper, and behind his head is a folded cape making a nimbus of brilliant, dazzling crimson. A symbol of his glory as a matador, the colour is soon to be appropriated by Doña Sol (Rita Hayworth), the free-loving society lady first seen striking a discordant note amid the soft blues and greens of the El Greco chapel as she sets her sights on Juan (Tyrone Power) while he prays before entering the ring. Before this, though, the scene of Juan's enthronement, composed with the vivid colours and movement of Titian.

A large, crowded room, bustling with activity and hung with gilt-framed portraits. At one end, raised on a platform, his chair draped with blue silk flowing handsomely to the floor, Juan sits bare-chested, the Titian flesh-tints

Blood and Sand: the robing of Juan. Tyrone Power, J. Carrol Naish and John Carradine

gradually clothed in the blue and gold brocades of his matador's costume. At the other, the attendants and the admirers patiently paying court. The camera pans slowly round in a circle from them to come to rest on Curro (Laird Cregar), the influential critic favoured with a seat in the centre of the room where – a red and gold matador's cape spread on his knees – he embarks on a soaring panegyric of Juan's art. The robing complete, everyone is asked to leave, and Curro whirls the cape round him in an exquisite pirouette (executed with astonishing grace by the massive Laird Cregar), leaving it to fall as a blood-red stain at Juan's feet. Left alone with the faithful Nacional (John Carradine), Juan confesses his fear: 'There's a feel of rust in my throat' – and again the crimson stain as Nacional holds the end of his sash and he pirouettes across the screen to wrap it round his waist and discover, not Nacional, but his wife Carmen (Linda Darnell), whom he will soon betray, now holding the other end.

Then, in the chapel, the meeting with Doña Sol; and in the ring as the corrida starts, a remarkable shot of her face, blood-red lips moistened, parting

Blood and Sand: Rita Hayworth and Linda Darnell

vampirically, as she leans forward literally drinking in Juan's fame and physique. 'If this is death in the afternoon,' says the cynical Curro, indicating the arena, 'she is death in the evening.' And, in the seduction scene later at her home, an elegant mansion of cool, marbled blues and whites, Mamoulian makes equally remarkable use of Velazquez space and light to set off the red and white chessmen, the red carnations on the table, which prelude the hard, predatory brilliance of her scarlet fingernails tapping on the guitar as she sings to Juan.

Counterpointing these illusory splendours, a motif of soft, romantic purity centering on Carmen, the patient Grizelda who is lent a touch of Juliet by being the object of two balcony serenades: the first as a child, when young Juan arrives by moonlight to announce his departure to Madrid, and makes an undignified exit by falling off the creeper which has carried him to her window; and the second when he arrives with a full orchestra to announce his return. Heralded twice by the moonlight, generally dressed in downy white with gentle mantillas softening the contours of her face, Carmen is as much an illusion as the glittering Doña Sol. Briefly, in her shortlived happiness with Juan, in her visit (dressed in unrelenting black) to plead her cause with Doña Sol, she becomes a woman. For the rest she is a wraith, haunting Juan's imagination as a dream of love, and haunting the ethereally tormented El Greco chapel where he faces his fears and finally meets his death.

If these twin motifs had been allowed to have the field to themselves, *Blood and Sand* might have been a masterpiece to match *Becky Sharp*. Unfortunately they are backed – or, rather, undermined – by several others, some good, some bad. The worst is the note of heavy foreboding introduced by Juan's mother, played by Nazimova as a *mater dolorosa*, usually seen on her knees gloomily scrubbing floors and for ever embarking on prophecies of doom as she recalls how she has seen it all before when Juan's father fell from fame to fear, and finally death. There is also the rather too pat circular construction, which has a matador named Garabato (J. Carrol Naish) riding the crest of the wave during Juan's boyhood; when Juan returns from Madrid, he is accosted by a beggar who turns out to be the same Garabato, and gives him a job as his dresser; and the circle is completed when Curro and Doña Sol, after Juan's fatal goring, grow ecstatic over the new and rising star of his rival, Manolo de Palma (Anthony Quinn). Rather better, mainly because of

Carradine's excellent performance, Nacional's grumbles about the bullring and his constant cry of 'This is my last season' as he struggles vainly to summon up the decision to quit.

With all of these dooms piling up – not to mention the sister and brother-in-law who batten on his earnings like vultures, and the numerous creditors who are more heard of than seen or felt – it is scarcely surprising that the film begins to founder. Nevertheless, for more than half its length, *Blood and Sand* is Mamoulian at his best, flowing easily along from the characteristic opening: a close-up of a poster, pan down, past a bull's head on the wall to a palliasse where young Juan lies sleepless, a sword on a cushion by his side. Suddenly he reaches for the sword, lunges at the bull's head and, ignoring his mother's drowsy 'Go to sleep!', slips out to the deserted alleyway and the turbulent café where Curro is laying down the law about the art of the matador. Following an argument with Curro (whose head he cracks a bottle over for insulting the memory of his father), one of those marvellous Mamoulian panoramas which began with the 'Isn't It Romantic?' sequence in *Love Me Tonight*: Juan fades out of the café, races through a silent forest, strips off his clothes, swims across a lake, pauses to steal a horse blanket at a gipsy encampment, and steals across the parapet of a deserted bullring where he calls softly to a lone bull waiting in the moonlight. Some lovely plunging shots of boy and bull prancing in the ring, watched from the distance by an elderly impresario who bows in graceful homage: 'Maestro, I am your unconditional admirer.'

Then the farewell to Carmen and the long march to Madrid, past Mamoulian's cat sitting on a milestone, ending (shades of *Love Me Tonight* again) with the footsore Juan standing heroically on the railway line, cape at the ready, as a train approaches: 'Have you ever seen a bull stop a train?' Here, and through the scenes of Juan's return to a brass band reception which turns out to be for someone else, the joyous *fiesta* to which he brings gifts for everybody, the preparations for his first major fight, the rhythms are fluid and impeccable. So, too, in the bullfighting sequences, which may not please *aficionados* with their use of long shots and doubles, but are superbly done: overhead shots down on the vast, impassive arena; nervous bustle outside the entrance doors, where cigarettes are hastily stubbed out, capes tossed into graceful folds, horses eased into position as the fanfare sounds; a shot inside the darkness of the pen as a square of light suddenly appears and the bull thunders out, hesitating in the sudden, dazzling sunlight.

Despite the mounting melodrama of the second half, leading to the inevitable goring of Juan and his death, *Blood and Sand* remains so intelligently designed that the basic motifs still work to a climax. Just as he maintained something in reserve for Garbo in *Queen Christina*, Mamoulian holds back the full emblazonment of Doña Sol till the moment of her betrayal in the café where she abandons Juan for Manolo's rising star. While Juan glowers, Manolo asks her to dance: 'I'd love to,' she answers, and throws off her shawl to reveal for the first time the full glory of her crimson evening gown. Returning to the chapel before his last corrida, Juan is haunted once more by the vision incarnate of Carmen, who hovers faithfully in the shadows to pray for him. And the last shot, as Manolo stands in the ring to acknowledge the roar of the crowd, is a slow pan across the arena, past a bouquet of trampled roses, to rest on a dull stain spreading in the sand.

14: *Rings on Her Fingers*

To work out his contract with Fox, Mamoulian made *Rings on Her Fingers*, a lightweight comedy about some amiable confidence tricksters hoist with their own petard, which turned out to be the only film he ever made in which one could not instantly recognise his hand. It is not so much that the film is bad – in fact, it is often elegant and amusing – as that it is un-Mamoulian in its reliance on dialogue. Possibly because he wasn't very interested, the film has no real rhythm, no visual motif, and can at best be described as second-rate Preston Sturges.

Spring Byington and Laird Cregar, engagingly teamed as the confidence tricksters, discover a pretty shop-girl whom they feel will suit their purpose nicely. 'We should have been born with blue blood,' they explain, 'so we have spent our lives correcting this biological error.' What they want her to do is find a millionaire, possibly but not necessarily handsome, marry him as soon as possible, and let everybody live happily ever after off the proceeds. When the shop-girl (Gene Tierney) expresses some doubt as to her competence to do what they ask, Cregar answers, unanswerably, 'What does one ask of a rose?' The sucker they pick out at a beach resort is handsome but not, as they believe, a millionaire. He (Henry Fonda) is a penniless clerk with a passion for yachts which leads to the misunderstanding. Fonda and Tierney naturally fall in love, have a mutual confession session, and decide to get married; and the rest of the film is devoted to the efforts of the two tricksters to blackmail Tierney (who hasn't confessed all) into ditching Fonda and marrying a genuine millionaire who is lined up and willing.

As with the Sturges films, the minor characters and their zany dialogue are often a delight. An old train conductor listens interestedly to the squabble as Fonda tries to work out how to support a wife on 65 dollars a week, angrily rejecting the suggestion that he might use her money (ill-gotten, as it happens); when they reach an agreement, the conductor beams paternally on them, 'I'm sure glad you got it patched up. But why don't you take the money?' A slot-machine attendant, asked 'Are you Nick?', promptly replies, 'Nah, I'm Chick. Nick's sick.' A railway station newsvendor watches with progressively mounting eyebrows as Tierney tries to maintain a romantic relationship with both Fonda and the millionaire in different parts of the same building. And, most Sturgian of all, the sad little bowler-hatted private eye who is saving up to build a cabin so that he can spend his retiring years duck-shooting, and meanwhile, dozing off on the job, happily mutters 'Bang! Bang!' to himself, no doubt dreaming of some heroic Philip Marlovian adventure.

Rings on Her Fingers: Henry Fonda and Gene Tierney with the private eye (Frank Orth)

Among the many genuinely funny gags: Laird Cregar, looming large in a swimming-costume and anxious not to be seen, sneaking like the cartoon Loopy de Loop from bush to bush, pursued by a small but persistent dog; a neat double-talk session with Fonda trying to describe the man who swindled him (Cregar), Tierney trying to confuse the issue, and the police officer finally snarling, 'I'm sending out this description: He's a tall short man with a bald bushy head of hair.' Or Fonda's last-minute rescue of Tierney, slouching hand-in-pocket, coat collar turned up, hat over eyes, in an imitation of Alan Ladd which has Laird Cregar cringing in terror, then, realising his mistake, airily sneering, 'Ye gods! Have you ever seen anything so corny?'

Fonda, brilliant throughout, also contributes a splendid sight gag in which he returns home drunk, lifts one foot to take off a shoe, falls back on the bed, curls up instantly fast asleep, and leaps energetically out of bed to start a new day when the alarm goes off a moment later. And he also makes the most of a neat running gag where, playing one-arm bandits and roulette tables which have secretly been fixed to let him win, he becomes convinced that his

Rings on Her Fingers: 'He's a tall man …'

mathematical genius has led him to an infallible formula: 'They're at my *mercy*!'
he gloats delightedly. Since both script and performances are unusually good,
one could cite other pleasing moments. In between, however, the film sags
distressingly – a rare complaint for a Mamoulian film – and is of only marginal
interest in his work.

Rings on Her Fingers: 'If I asked for a waltz, they'd knife me ...'

15: *Summer Holiday*

For the next five years, Mamoulian worked exclusively for the stage, producing four musicals in a row: *Oklahoma!*, *Sadie Thompson*, *Carousel* and *St Louis Woman*. With the exception of *Meet Me in St. Louis* and Henry King's charming Charleston and raccoon-coated *Margie*, those were lean years in the cinema for the intimate as opposed to the production-number musical; but 1947 was the *annus mirabilis* which brought both *The Pirate* and *Summer Holiday*, each perfect in its own way, and sharing a common denominator in that neither used song and dance as decoration, but rather as part of the basic narrative structure.

Summer Holiday, indeed, uses both even more radically, with the irresistible gaiety of its songs, polkas and hayride dances forming a bedrock for the basic concept of *Ah, Wilderness!*, the Eugene O'Neill play on which it is based. *Ah, Wilderness!* is the exception to the rule of towering tragedy in O'Neill's work, a tender, nostalgic comedy in which he recalled (semi-autobiographically) and gently satirised the growing pains of adolescence. 'My purpose,' he wrote, 'was to write a play true to the spirit of the American large small-town at the turn of the century. Its quality depended upon atmosphere, sentiment, an exact evocation of the mood of a dead past.' He did so, of course, through dialogue and characterisation. Yet he was also strongly aware of the evocative power of popular music. Witness his use of the shanty 'Shenandoah' in *Mourning Becomes Electra*, and a similar employment of songs to stir the emotions in several of his plays, including *The Hairy Ape*, *All God's Chillun Got Wings* and *The Iceman Cometh*. Witness also a semi-humorous poem he once wrote about his musical tastes:

The long-haired high-brows call me 'vulgarian'
When the 'Great Big Beautiful Doll' I croon
For I'm strong for the music that's real American
And the joy of my heart is a rag time tune.

Nothing, in fact, could be more quintessentially O'Neill – who always had to labour so hard for his atmosphere amid a plethora of adjectives and exclamation-marks – than the 'Weary Blues' sung in the film by Marilyn Maxwell as the saloon girl who gives young Richard Miller his first taste of sin: with its age-old, yearning lament for hope and disillusionment, it almost sums up the whole of *Anna Christie*.

In the play, the 'spirit of the American small-town', dependent on warm ensemble playing by the cast, emerges slowly through the family feeling gradually engendered by O'Neill's dialogue. In the film, it is instantly present as Walter Huston (playing Nat Miller, newspaper proprietor and paterfamilias) is discovered in his office, standing in front of a wall map of America and embarking on his recitative song, 'Our Town', which describes the humble virtues of the Danville of 1906: 'Our town isn't found on the map / Though we're part of Connecticut.' As he continues the description of the town and his home, a dissolve takes him to a quiet, tree-lined avenue; entering a neat front gate, he interjects a snatch of dialogue as his youngest son tears busily past, continues the song as he enters the house to encounter his eldest son and daughter just going out, and ends it precisely at the moment when he opens the kitchen door on his wife. They talk of the impending departure of Uncle Sid, who enters on cue to ask 'Where's Lily?' and the camera follows him to the dining room where Lily is crossly packing heart-shaped cookies for his trip and muttering 'I can't forget that woman in New York.' 'Where's Richard?' Uncle Sid asks. Cut on the reply, 'Off with that McComber girl', to a drugstore where Richard and his girl Muriel, sharing one soda with two straws, discuss life and find themselves finishing the 'Our Town' song.

The sequence is exemplary in every way: in its fluid, graceful movement which whisks one through the town and the Miller home; in its introduction of all the principal characters without seeming to go out of its way to do so; in the quick character sketches, of the awful youngest child, the superciliously

Summer Holiday: 'Afraid to Fall in Love': Mickey Rooney and Gloria De Haven; the Independence Day picnic

almost-adult older ones, the adolescent pretensions of Richard; in the touch of naturalism superimposed on the stylisation by the fact that Huston uses his own rough voice for the song; and above all in the hint of time embalmed by memory, confirmed later, through the abortive romance between feckless, drunken Uncle Sid and prim Aunt Lily, which has obviously been on and off for years and will continue so for years more as one of those hallowed family traditions unchanged by the business of growing up.

The spirit of the small town, of time remembered, is thus securely established. All that remains is to give it flesh by setting it down in the green and pleasant land of fond recollection, which is instantly done. As Richard and Muriel finish their soda and the song, she says 'I gotta go', he says 'Let's walk through the park', and Mamoulian dissolves to them strolling through a leafy terrace in the bright summer evening. Richard talks dreamily about the graduation day speech he is preparing: 'I'm going to say things that are positively revolutionary.' Then he adds, 'My mind's made up, I'm going to live. Have a jelly bean?', and he tries to kiss her. She baulks, he sings 'Why Should Anybody Be Afraid?' 'I'm not afraid,' she cries, taking up the song, and as he tries to kiss her again, they are suddenly whisked into a joyous polka across a dazzling expanse of grass that is greener than green.

The advantage Mamoulian has over O'Neill is that he can *show* the world of nostalgia instead of merely suggesting it: the radiantly green lawns which are inseparable from summer and young love, not as they were but as they are remembered; the rows of ideally clean, bright and hopeful faces at the Graduation Day ceremony; the little street tidy and expectant with its rows of flags awaiting Independence Day. Oddly enough the film is least successful in one brief sequence where it attempts to recreate too faithfully in a series of tableaux vivants based on famous paintings by Grant Wood ('Daughters of the American Revolution'), Thomas Benton and John Curry; most successful when creating a pure Utopia of endless summer days, green grass, flowing meadows and simple pleasures in an untroubled land of peace and plenty. Central to this vision is the superb Independence Day picnic sequence which effortlessly conjures up the paradise imagined by Kubla Khan as the setting for his stately pleasure dome:

Summer Holiday: dance at the picnic

And there were gardens bright with sinuous rills
Where blossomed many an incense-bearing tree;
And here were forests ancient as the hills,
Enfolding sunny spots of greenery.

The sequence begins with a rush of excitement as everyone heads for the picnic ground. Close-up of a trumpeter sweating profusely in his tight scarlet and gold uniform, getting redder and redder as he strains to hit a high note; track back to take in the whole tableau of the bandstand; then a whole series of brief, apparently random shots, linked by dissolves and fast pans, which somehow dovetail into a perfectly choreographed dance. The beer wagons arriving with supplies; men cheering on a drinking contest, ladies indulging in a game of croquet; tables laden with food; small boys darting in hopefully; a violinist and three girls on a grassy slope; a circle of dancers run in, are instantly

metamorphosed into a square dance, then circle off as a crocodile in overhead shot while a dissolve returns to the drinking contest and its end in the collapse of all three surviving competitors. Cut to Mrs Miller in the hall welcoming her family back one by one in various states of inebriation and exhilaration. 'Have you had a nice day?' she asks. 'No,' says Richard gloomily.

One of the complaints frequently laid against *Summer Holiday* is that it robs O'Neill's play of much of its warmth and genuine feeling by allowing Mickey Rooney to play the part of Richard Miller, the rebellious and impossibly arty adolescent, chiefly for farce. Actually, his cheerfully strident interpretation of the role as a minimal variant on Andy Hardy works remarkably well, despite the anachronism of his enthusiasms for Swinburne, Omar Khayyám and Carlyle's *French Revolution*, and despite the fact that he seems hardly likely to develop into the writer-poet envisaged by O'Neill. The yearning arrogance of adolescence, after all, doesn't change all that much from

Summer Holiday: Gloria De Haven, Mickey Rooney and Agnes Moorehead launch the Stanley Steamer song

generation to generation; and with so much built-in sentiment present in the settings, songs and dances, his stridency is probably useful as a doorstop to prevent the film from succumbing to the ever-present danger attendant upon nostalgia: sentimentality.

The criticism, in any case, seems to miss the point of the film. Unlike *Meet Me in St. Louis*, *Summer Holiday* is not simply a tender evocation of family life from a gentler, more leisurely age. It is an attempt to pin down that moment which comes in everyone's life when one sees things from a new perspective: you realise that your schooldays probably were the happiest days of your life even though you hated every moment of them; or that you loved your family even though you couldn't wait to leave home; or that the world is a marvellous place even if it seems to have no use for you. Despite his momentary pleasures (the splendid 'Stanley Steamer' song, when he is allowed to drive his father's steam-powered car, with the entire family – even Aunt Lily – joining in), Richard wanders through the film with his eyes, memory and sensibilities closed, so intent on the private fantasy he is building about life that he sees nothing, understands nothing. He is narcissistic in his relationship with Muriel; he is patronising in his treatment of both the town and everybody he meets; he is unbelievably pompous in the revolutionary inanities of his graduation day speech. Finally, however, his ego takes a severe beating in the marvellous sequence of his encounter with the saloon girl Belle, several inches taller than he is, who becomes redder and redder and more and more alarming as he becomes drunker and drunker and more deeply embroiled in sins which are right out of his depth.

Then comes the splendid moment of illumination. Father and son have just had one of those man-to-man talks about the facts of life and loose women, with Mickey Rooney watching in distress as Walter Huston agitatedly crushes his clay sculpture of Abraham Lincoln out of all recognition while trying to find the right words about what happened with Belle that night in the saloon; Rooney finally puts him out of his misery by announcing that he has learned his lesson and that what he really wants to do is marry Muriel. It is evening. Uncle Sid and Aunt Lily sit romantically at peace with the world in a swing chair out in the moonlit garden. Nat, watching from the window, says to his wife, 'We seem to be completely surrounded by love', and as Richard comes down on his way out to see Muriel, he recalls the days of his own courtship. Suddenly touched, Richard darts forward and kisses them both. Pleased but startled, Nat watches him go out: 'First time he's done that in years. I don't believe in kissing between father and son ... but that *meant* something.' Outside, as Richard pauses in the street, the moment is sealed by a magnificent crane shot up past him, past Lily and Sid, past Nat and his wife as they stand on their balcony looking down over (as Nat puts it) 'Love's young dream'.

Beautifully shot by Charles Schoenbaum in warm, soft colours, *Summer Holiday* equals *Love Me Tonight* in the mastery with which rhymed dialogue, songs and leisurely action are swept up by Mamoulian's cutting into one dynamic overall rhythm. It is with some surprise that one realises in examining the film in detail that, despite some admirable steps created by Charles Walters, there are really no formal dance numbers in the film at all. Mamoulian needs neither dances nor dancers to create choreography; but when he did finally use them, ten years later in *Silk Stockings*, the result was arguably his greatest film.

16: *Silk Stockings*

After *Summer Holiday*, which was not exactly a success (a hostile British press was spearheaded by C. A. Lejeune in the *Observer*, who called it 'A degrading film'), Mamoulian suffered a second long exile, again spent in the theatre, where he re-staged *Oklahoma!* and *Carousel*, and produced two new musicals and one straight play. It was almost ten years before he came back to the cinema with *Silk Stockings*, an adaptation of the Cole Porter musical which derived in its turn from Lubitsch's *Ninotchka*, the film in which Garbo, according to erroneous legend, graced the screen with her laugh for the first time as the glamorous Russian commissar who falls in love with a capitalist in Paris and is forced to choose between love and duty.

Summer Holiday had at least been stoutly defended by *Sequence*; but this time no champion was forthcoming, and *Silk Stockings* was summarily dismissed amid a flurry of crocodile tears about East–West relations and some starry-eyed but irrelevant recollections of Garbo. 'Cyd Charisse, as Ninotchka, is no Garbo,' complained the *Observer*, blithely ignoring the fact that she wasn't meant to be. To draw comparisons between *Silk Stockings* and *Ninotchka* is as fruitless an occupation as complaining that *Kiss Me Kate* isn't *The Taming of the Shrew*, or, for that matter, that *Summer Holiday* isn't *Ah! Wilderness*. Much more to the point is the way in which Mamoulian has improved on the stage version by giving it an emotional depth in line with the original.

Broadly speaking, the stage musical follows the plot of the Lubitsch film fairly closely. Ninotchka still comes to Paris to discipline three defecting envoys, and she still falls in love with her decadent Western charmer. Their

mission, however, is no longer to get money for tractors by selling some Grand Ducal jewellery, but to coax a wandering composer back to Moscow; and her seducer is no longer a French aristocrat but a Hollywood film director. These changes, together with the introduction of 'America's swimming sweetheart', the glamorous star about to appear in her first serious, non-swimming film, provide the basis for a trio of show-biz songs which turn the satire against Hollywood as much as against Communism; while the love affair, started as a witty fencing match in such songs as 'Paris Loves Lovers', 'It's a Chemical Reaction, That's All', and 'All of You', is sealed in Ninotchka's mournful 'Without Love' and a lightweight romantic duet called 'As on Through the Seasons We Sail' ('When we are man and wife/I swear to make our life/A revolutionary fairy-tale'), neither of which stirs any very deep emotions.

Mamoulian, while remaining very faithful to the stage version, made several important changes because, as he put it (interview with Douchet and Tavernier in *Positif*), 'I had two of the best dancers in the world, and what

Silk Stockings 'All of You'. Fred Astaire and Cyd Charisse

interested me was to give greater importance to the dancing than to the action proper, which was merely a repeat of *Ninotchka*. The psychological and dramatic development existed only in the dances. It was by dancing that the characters became aware of something or other ...' There is a wonderful moment like this when love first dawns on Cyd Charisse's Ninotchka. Steve Canfield (Astaire) has at last found an opportunity to get her alone in order to make his romantic pitch. Interested but hardly helpful ('The arrangement of your features is not entirely repulsive to me'), Ninotchka brings out her little black book to make notes and embarks on her exposition of Kamachev's theory of love:

If the electro-magnetic of the he-male
Meets the electro-magnetic of the female
If right away she should say
This is the male
It's a chemical reaction, that's all.

Exasperated, Canfield counters with his theory that there is no theory:

I love the looks of you
The lure of you
I'd love to make
A tour of you
The arms, the eyes,
The mouth of you
The East, West, North
And the South of you.

The two songs overlap, with Canfield winning as he begins to illustrate his theory in dance, first with a pirouette, then a joyous little tap dance in an attempt to get her to let herself go. 'You go, go, go, but you don't get anywhere,' she says scornfully. 'You're telling me,' says Canfield and resumes his dance with a chair. Suddenly, he pulls the surprised Ninotchka up into his arms; and as the music swells into full-throated orchestration for the first time, her leg curves almost involuntarily into a perfect arabesque, and she is whirled off, transformed, into the dance. The moment has the same thrill of magic as that felt by Frankenstein in Mary Shelley's novel when he watched for that first spark of life which he felt would 'pour a torrent of light into our dark world'. The dance over, Canfield gently teases her about her new-found ability to dance. 'Once,' she begins to explain dreamily, 'a few years ago …', then breaks off to become the stiff commissar once more; but one knows, in spite of the reappearance of the little black book in which she annotates Canfield's kiss, that she has both come irrevocably alive and fallen irrevocably in love.

Since their emotion is expressed in movement rather than words, the 'As on Through the Seasons We Sail' song has accordingly been cut, and Mamoulian pulls off his master stroke by changing the 'Silk Stockings' number from a song by Canfield into a dance by Ninotchka. Immediately following her dance with Canfield, Ninotchka is seen at her typewriter, dreamily typing to the rhythm of 'I Love the Looks of You' instead of rattling like a machine gun as previously. She goes to speak to the composer, Boroff, and finds him being entertained at a fashion show by America's swimming sweetheart. 'Tell me, comrade,' she says, 'when a woman wears things like that is it really so attractive to a man?' 'In a word,' says Boroff enthusiastically, 'Da!' In the stage version, when Ninotchka subsequently appears in her new, secretly acquired finery and Canfield sings his appreciation in 'Silk Stockings', it is little more than a neat capping of the earlier joke when Ninotchka, gazing at a window display of lingerie and adapting Garbo's line about the hat, exclaimed in prim disgust, 'How can such a civilisation survive which permits women to wear things like these?' In the film, it is much more. We watch Ninotchka dressing for her date with Canfield, and her slow, dreamy dance as she casts away her old clothes and lovingly draws out her silk stockings, earrings, filmy underwear and high heels one by one from their secret hiding-places all over the apartment, is as much an affirmation of love as the bedroom-stroking sequence in *Queen Christina* on which it is obviously patterned. And the finality of the gesture with which, once dressed and radiant in her silks and satins, she tosses her old black stockings away on to a chair, is curiously reminiscent in its

Silk Stockings: 'How can such a civilisation survive …'

self-abandonment of the moment when Christina slips off her doublet and waits for Antonio to acknowledge her femininity.

'One's heart doesn't break for Cyd Charisse as it broke for Garbo,' the *Sunday Times* review complained. On the contrary, it does, but only if one realises that the equivalent of Garbo-Ninotchka's face in close-up is not Charisse-Ninotchka's expression but her movement. Compare, for instance, her dancing in the joyous 'Fated to Be Mated' number which goes airily into orbit through a series of deserted sets in a film studio just before her discovery of what she supposes to be Canfield's betrayal, and the mechanical gaiety of

the 'Red Blues' number in which, back in Moscow, she and her friends pay homage to their memories of the decadent West. It isn't just that all life and colour have been drained away – instead of the fishnets, fountains and railway platforms of the studio sets, a vast, bare hall; instead of the bright kaleidoscope of colours, nothing but mournful greys, blues and khaki-browns: Ninotchka herself has become an automaton, dancing not out of exhilaration but as though discharging a duty.

After the 'Red Blues' number and Canfield's successful manoeuvres to get Ninotchka sent back to Paris from Moscow, the stage version rather petered out in a finale which simply reprised 'Too bad, we couldn't stay in Moscow.' The film, by one of those happy accidents or instinctively right choices, completes its unfinished emotional line with 'The Ritz Roll'n Rock', a solo dance with chorus line for Fred Astaire. Astaire, in his autobiography, *Steps in Time*, has recorded how he felt (quite rightly) that he needed 'a sock solo' at this point, and asked Cole Porter to write a rock and roll number. Porter, after listening to a few appropriate records, did so, and the result, choreographed by Astaire and Hermes Pan, is one of Astaire's most brilliant virtuoso numbers for top hat, white tie and cane. His personality so dominates both stage and dance that the ending of the film is ready-made. Canfield returns to his dressing room to find the puzzled Ninotchka waiting and wondering why she has been sent back to Paris. When he explains that he engineered it because he wanted to marry her, she is completely vanquished. 'You!' she says, making him a gift of her electromagnetic formula. 'Come here!' Anything else would have been tautological, and the film ends on their kiss and a delighted chorus of 'Too bad, we can't go back to Moscow' from the three Russians.

Quite apart from its use of dance to narrate the progress of the love story, *Silk Stockings* is so rich in invention that it gives the lie even more forcefully than *The Mark of Zorro*, *Blood and Sand* or *Summer Holiday* to the myth of Mamoulian's decline. Right from the opening his inimitable touch is evident in the series of foot-level shots which tracks Canfield from his room across a corridor, into a lift, pause to stare at a pair of pretty female feet, out of the hotel, into a taxi, and up the stage-door steps to the theatre where Boroff, just finishing a concert and having received a telegram summoning him back to Moscow, divides his time between threatening to commit suicide and dashing

Silk Stockings: sock solo for Astaire: 'The Ritz Roll'n Rock'

(*next page*) *Silk Stockings*: Astaire, Janis Paige and boardroom table

back on stage to keep the applause up to scratch. From there on, with some of Cole Porter's best numbers impeccably staged and looking as though they had been poured into the story, we are unquestionably watching a Mamoulian film. The ease with which he slips in and out of dialogue sequences and into musical numbers without any perceptible faltering in rhythm is incredible, as is the constant invention he brings to the action. The wonderful shot, for instance, in which he adds his own gloss to 'Stereophonic Sound', the number celebrating Hollywood's mania for CinemaScope, colour and, of course, stereophonic sound: Astaire and Janis Paige suddenly leap headlong on to a boardroom table, sliding towards each other from opposite ends with hands outstretched ... and just, but only just, meet across the vast expanse of the CinemaScope screen. Or the opening track in through the ladies and gentlemen of Napoleon's court to a close shot of Janis Paige as she embarks on her wonderfully vulgar 'Josephine' number; and, once the horrified Ninotchka has put a stop to this butchery of Boroff's music, the way the deserted set is used for the 'Siberia' lament sung by the three chastened envoys.

Silk Stockings: Peter Lorre, Astaire, Joseph Buloff and Jules Munshin with Betty Utti, Tybee Afra and Barrie Chase in 'Too bad ...'

Silk Stockings, in fact, is so crammed with delights that it seems incredible that anybody, let alone the entire pack of British critics, should have failed to respond. The catalogue is endless. Janis Paige as the swimming sweetheart, for ever tapping hopefully at a waterlogged ear and responding to every question involving a name (even Tolstoy's) with an automatic 'There is absolutely *no* truth to the rumours; we're just good friends'; Peter Lorre as the shortest, plumpest and most sinful of the three envoys, generally to be seen in a corner happily performing a Russian dance propped up by chairs, and confirming their final defection with a gleeful 'We are now rotten capitalists, and if all goes well, we'll be much more rotten than we ever dreamed'; George Tobias as the newly instated commissar who watches his predecessor being marched out and then picks up the phone to ask, 'Does this office have a copy of *Who's Still Who?*' Above all, with its generous allowance of thirteen musical numbers, ranging from the enchanting 'Paris Loves Lovers' to the brassy 'Satin and Silk', *Silk Stockings* is enormously cheerful and cheering. And as Ninotchka gloomily puts it, 'Nobody can be so happy without being punished.' This, to date, is Mamoulian's last film. Perhaps, one day, critics, historians and those who write about the cinema will at last realise that it is one of the great musicals.

Notes

1. As described by Mamoulian: 'To accompany the transformations I wanted a completely unrealistic sound. First I tried rhythmic beats, like a heartbeat. We tried every sort of drum, but they all sounded like drums. Then I recorded my own heart beating, and it was perfect, marvellous. Then we recorded a gong, took off the actual impact noise, and reversed the reverberations. Finally we painted on the soundtrack; and I think that was the first time anyone had used synthetic sound like that, working from light to sound.'
2. 'Like Ordinary People Do', 'You're the Cats', 'Nobody Loves a Riveter'.
3. '… to my mind it's a sonnet. It was done to a metronome. I explained to her: "This has to be sheer poetry and feeling. The movement must be like a dance. Treat it the way you would do it to music."'
4. Commenting on the film during a screening at the National Film Theatre in April 1968, Mamoulian described how this scene was shot in summer, with oatmeal standing in for snow, and how Garbo, a non-smoker, was persuaded to take a single puff so that her breath would have the correct frosty look. In the subsequent scene of the French ambassador's presentation, Garbo was to be flanked by two huge dogs who were to be as remote and uninterested as she. Mamoulian tried to solve the problem of keeping them still by perching a cat on the ambassador's shoulder (out of camera range). The cat was uncooperative, but the dogs brought their own solution by staring fixedly at the ambassador's periwig, under the impression that it was the cat.
5. After the termination of her Goldwyn contract, Anna Sten continued to appear in films, mostly of no great distinction, up to 1962. Recently she has devoted herself mainly to painting.

Filmography

ROUBEN MAMOULIAN

Born Tbilisi, Georgia (Russia), 8 October 1898.
Studied at the Universities of Moscow and London, and the Vakhtangov Studio
of the Moscow Art Theatre. Went to America in 1923.

FEATURES

Applause (1929)

PRODUCTION COMPANY	Paramount
PRODUCERS	Jesse L. Lasky, Walter Wanger
DIRECTOR	Rouben Mamoulian
SCRIPT	Garrett Fort. Based on the novel by Beth Brown
DIRECTOR OF PHOTOGRAPHY	George Folsey
EDITOR	John Bassler
SONGS	

'What Wouldn't I Do For
That Man?' . . . . .E. Y. Harburg and Jay Gorney; sung by
Helen Morgan;
'Give Your Little Baby Lots
of Lovin'' . . . . .Dolly Morse and Joe Burke; sung by Helen
Morgan
Also, 'Pretty Baby', 'Waiting for the Robert E. Lee', 'The Turkey Trot', 'I've
Got a Feelin' I'm Fallin'', 'Yaaka Hula Hickey Dula'

SOUND . . . . .Ernest F. Zatorsky

Helen Morgan (Kitty Darling), Joan Peers (April Darling), Fuller Mellish, Jr (Hitch Nelson), Henry Wadsworth (Tony), Jack Cameron (Joe King), Dorothy Cumming.

Filmed in the Astoria Studios, New York, and on location in New York.
Released in US, 4 January 1930; UK, 28 April 1930.
Running time: 82 mins (US), 80 mins (UK).
DISTRIBUTORS Paramount.

City Streets (1931)

PRODUCTION COMPANY . . . . . .Paramount
DIRECTOR . . . . .Rouben Mamoulian
SCRIPT . . . . .Max Marcin, Oliver H. P. Garrett. Based on
a story by Dashiell Hammett
ADAPTATION . . . . .Max Marcin
DIRECTOR OF PHOTOGRAPHY . .Lee Garmes
MUSIC/ORCHESTRATION . . . . . .Sidney Cutner
SOUND . . . . .J. A. Goodrich, M. M. Paggi

Gary Cooper (The Kid), Sylvia Sidney (Nan), Paul Lukas (Big Fella Maskal), Guy Kibbee (Pop Cooley), William Boyd (McCoy), Wynne Gibson (Agnes), Betty Sinclair (Pansy), Stanley Fields (Blackie).

Filmed in the Paramount Studios, Hollywood.
Released in US, 18 April 1931; UK, 9 August 1931. Running time: 74 mins.
DISTRIBUTORS Paramount.

Dr Jekyll and Mr Hyde (1931)

PRODUCTION COMPANY . . . . . .Paramount
PRODUCER . . . . .Rouben Mamoulian
DIRECTOR . . . . .Rouben Mamoulian

SCRIPT .Samuel Hoffenstein, Percy Heath. Based on
the novel by Robert Louis Stevenson
DIRECTOR OF PHOTOGRAPHY . .Karl Struss
ART DIRECTOR . . . . .Hans Dreier
SONG
'Champagne Ivy' . . . . .Sung by Miriam Hopkins
PIANO MUSIC . . . . .Schumann's 'Aufschwung'

Fredric March (Dr Henry Jekyll/Mr Hyde), Miriam Hopkins (Ivy Pearson),
Rose Hobart (Muriel Carew), Holmes Herbert (Dr Lanyon), Edgar Norton
(Poole), Halliwell Hobbes (Brig.-Gen. Carew), Arnold Lucy (Utterson),
Tempe Pigott (Mrs Hawkins), Colonel McDonnell (Hobson).

Filmed in the Paramount Studios, Hollywood.
Released in US, 2 January 1932; UK, 11 February 1932.
Running time: 90 mins (US), 81 mins (UK).
DISTRIBUTORS Paramount.

Love Me Tonight (1932)

PRODUCTION COMPANY . . . . . .Paramount
PRODUCER . . . . .Rouben Mamoulian
DIRECTOR . . . . .Rouben Mamoulian
SCRIPT .Samuel Hoffenstein, Waldemar Young,
George Marion, Jr. Based on a play by
Leopold Marchand, Paul Armont
DIRECTOR OF PHOTOGRAPHY . .Victor Milner
ART DIRECTOR . . . . .Hans Dreier
SONGS .Richard Rodgers and Lorenz Hart
'The Song of Paree' . . . . .Sung by Maurice Chevalier
'How Are You?' . . . . .Sung by Maurice Chevalier
'Isn't It Romantic?' . . . . .Sung by Maurice Chevalier, Bert Roach,
Rolf Sedan, Tyler Brooke, Jeanette
MacDonald

'Lover' .Sung by Jeanette MacDonald
'Mimi' .Sung by Maurice Chevalier, C. Aubrey
Smith, Charles Ruggles, Charles
Butterworth, Elizabeth Patterson, Ethel
Griffies, Blanche Frederici
'A Woman Needs Something
Like That' . . . . .Sung/spoken by Joseph Cawthorn, Jeanette
MacDonald
'Poor Apache' . . . . .Sung by Maurice Chevalier
'Love Me Tonight' . . . . .Sung by Jeanette MacDonald, Maurice
Chevalier
'The Son of a Gun is Nothing
But a Tailor' . . . . .Sung by C. Aubrey Smith, Robert Greig,
Cecil Cunningham, Marion Byron, Edgar
Norton, Rita Owin, George Humbert

Jeanette MacDonald (Princess Jeanette), Maurice Chevalier (Maurice
Courtelin), Charles Ruggles (Vicomte Gilbert de Vareze), Charles
Butterworth (Count de Savignac), Sir C. Aubrey Smith (The Duke), Myrna
Loy (Valentine), Elizabeth Patterson (1st Aunt), Ethel Griffies (2nd Aunt),
Blanche Frederici (3rd Aunt), Joseph Cawthorn (Doctor), Robert Greig
(Majordomo), Ethel Wales (Dressmaker), Marion Byron (Bakery Girl), Mary
Doran (Mme Dupont), Bert Roach (Emile), Cecil Cunningham (Laundress),
Tyler Brooke (Composer), Edgar Norton (Valet), Herbert Mundin (Groom),
Rita Owin (Chambermaid), Clarence Wilson (Shirtmaker), Gordon Westcott
(Collector), George Davis (Pierre), Rolf Sedan (Taxi driver), Tony Merio
(Hatmaker), William H. Turner (Bootmaker), George 'Gabby' Hayes
(Grocer), George Humbert (Chef).

Filmed in the Paramount Studios, Hollywood.
First shown in US, 18 August 1932; UK, 17 November 1932.
Running time: 90 mins.
DISTRIBUTORS Paramount.

Song of Songs (1933)

PRODUCTION COMPANY	Paramount
PRODUCER	Rouben Mamoulian
DIRECTOR	Rouben Mamoulian
SCRIPT	Leo Birinski, Samuel Hoffenstein. Based on the novel *Das hohe Lied* by Hermann Sudermann and the play by Edward Sheldon
DIRECTOR OF PHOTOGRAPHY	Victor Milner
ART DIRECTOR	Hans Dreier
MUSIC	Karl Hajos, Milan Rodern
MUSICAL DIRECTOR	Nathaniel W. Finston
SONGS	
'Heidenröslein'	Franz Schubert; sung by Marlene Dietrich
'Johnny'	Friedrich Holländer and Edward Hayman; sung by Marlene Dietrich
COSTUMES	Travis Banton
SCULPTURES	S. C. Scarpitta

Marlene Dietrich (Lily), Brian Aherne (Richard Waldow), Lionel Atwill (Baron von Merzbach), Alison Skipworth (Mrs Rasmussen), Hardie Albright (Edward von Prell), Helen Freeman (Miss von Schwertfeger), Richard Bennett, James Marcus, Morgan Wallace, Wilson Benge, Hans Schumm.

Filmed in the Paramount Studios, Hollywood.
Released in US, July 1933; UK, 26 September 1933.
Running time: 83 mins. [A song, 'You Are My Song of Songs' by Ralph Rainger and Leo Robin, was cut from all release prints.]
DISTRIBUTORS Paramount.

Queen Christina (1933)

PRODUCTION COMPANY	MGM
PRODUCER	Walter Wanger
DIRECTOR	Rouben Mamoulian

SCRIPT .Salka Viertel, H. M. Harwood. Based on an
original story by Salka Viertel, Margaret P.
Levine
DIALOGUE . . . . .S. N. Behrman
DIRECTOR OF PHOTOGRAPHY . .William Daniels
EDITOR . . . . .Blanche Sewell
ART DIRECTOR . . . . .Alexander Toluboff, Edwin B. Willis
MUSIC .Herbert Stothart
COSTUMES . . . . .Adrian
SOUND .Douglas Shearer

Greta Garbo (Christina), John Gilbert (Antonio), Ian Keith (Magnus), Lewis
Stone (Oxenstierna), Elizabeth Young (Ebba), Sir C. Aubrey Smith (Aage),
Reginald Owen (Prince Charles), George Renevent (French Ambassador),
Gustav von Seyffertitz (General), David Torrence (Archbishop), Ferdinand
Munier (Innkeeper), Akim Tamiroff (Pedro), Cora Sue Collins (Christina as
a child), Edward Norris, Lawrence Grant.

Filmed in the MGM Studios, Hollywood.
Released in US, December 1933; UK, 16 February 1934. Running time: 100 mins.
DISTRIBUTORS MGM.

We Live Again (1934)

PRODUCTION COMPANY . . . . . .Samuel Goldwyn
PRODUCER . . . . .Samuel Goldwyn
DIRECTOR . . . . .Rouben Mamoulian
ASSISTANT DIRECTOR . . . . .Robert Lee
SCRIPT .Leonard Praskins. Based on the novel
Voskresonie [*Resurrection*] by Leo Tolstoy
ADAPTATION . . . . .Maxwell Anderson, Leonard Praskins,
Preston Sturges
DIRECTOR OF PHOTOGRAPHY . .Gregg Toland
EDITOR . . . . .Otho Lovering
PRODUCTION DESIGNER . . . . . .Sergei Sudeikin

```
ART DIRECTOR  . . . . . . . . . . . . .Richard Day
MUSIC/MUSICAL DIRECTOR  . . . .Alfred Newman
ORCHESTRATIONS  . . . . . . . . . .Edward Powell
COSTUMES . . . . . . . . . . . . . . . . .Omar Kiam
SOUND . . . . . . . . . . . . . . . . . . . .Frank Maher
```

Anna Sten (Katusha Maslova), Fredric March (Prince Dmitri Nekhlyudov), Jane Baxter (Missy Kortchagin), Sir C. Aubrey Smith (Prince Kortchagin), Ethel Griffies (Aunt Marie), Gwendolyn Logan (Aunt Sophia), Jessie Ralph (Matrona Pavlovna), Sam Jaffe (Simonson), Cecil Cunningham (Theodosia), Dale Fuller (Euphemia Botchkova), Leonid Kinsky (Simon Kartinkin), Mary Forbes (Princess Kortchagin), Jessie Arnold (Korablova), Fritzi Ridgeway (The Red Head), Morgan Wallace (The Colonel), Davison Clark (Tikhon), Michael Visaroff and Edgar Norton (Judges), Crauford Kent.

Released in US, 16 November 1934; UK, 5 November 1934.
Running time: 84 mins.
DISTRIBUTORS United Artists.

Becky Sharp (1935)

```
PRODUCTION COMPANY  . . . . . .Pioneer Pictures
PRODUCER  . . . . . . . . . . . . . . . .Kenneth Macgowan
DIRECTOR . . . . . . . . . . . . . . . . .Rouben Mamoulian
ASSISTANT DIRECTOR . . . . . . . . .Argyle Nelson
SCRIPT . . . . . . . . . . . . . . . . . . . .Francis Edward Faragoh. Based on the play
                                         by Langdon Mitchell adapted from the novel
                                         Vanity Fair by W. M. Thackeray
DIRECTOR OF PHOTOGRAPHY . .Ray Rennahan
COLOUR PROCESS . . . . . . . . . . . .Technicolor
TECHNICOLOR DIRECTOR  . . . . .Natalie Kalmus
EDITOR  . . . . . . . . . . . . . . . . . . .Archie Marshek
PRODUCTION DESIGNER  . . . . . .Robert Edmond Jones
ASSOCIATE ART DIRECTOR  . . . .W. B. Ihnen
MUSIC  . . . . . . . . . . . . . . . . . . . .Roy Webb
```

SONG

'The Lass With the Delicate Air' Sung by Miriam Hopkins

CHOREOGRAPHY ....Russell Lewis

SOUND ....Earl A. Wolcott

Miriam Hopkins (Becky Sharp), Sir Cedric Hardwicke (Marquis of Steyne), Nigel Bruce (Joseph Sedley), Frances Dee (Amelia Sedley), Alan Mowbray (Rawdon Crawley), G. P. Huntley, Jr (George Osborne), George Hassell (Sir Pitt Crawley), William Stack (Pitt Crawley), Colin Tapley (William Dobbin), William Faversham (Duke of Wellington), Alison Skipworth (Miss Julia Crawley), Billie Burke (Lady Bareacres), Charles Richman (General Tufto), Doris Lloyd (Duchess of Richmond), Leonard Mudie (Tarquin), Bunny Beatty (Lady Blanche), Charles Coleman (Bowles), May Beatty (Briggs), Finis Barton (Miss Flowery), Olaf Hytten (The Prince Regent), Pauline Garon (Fifine), James 'Hambone' Robinson (Page), Elspeth Dudgeon (Miss Pinkerton), Tempe Pigott (The Charwoman), Ottola Nesmith (Lady Jane Crawley).

Filming began on 3 December 1934 under the direction of Lowell Sherman, who died on 28 December. Filming resumed from scratch on 14 January 1935 with Mamoulian as director.

Released in US, 28 June 1935; UK, 11 July 1935. Running time: 84 mins.

DISTRIBUTORS RKO Radio.

The Gay Desperado (1936)

PRODUCTION COMPANY ......Pickford-Lasky

PRODUCERS ....Mary Pickford, Jesse L. Lasky

PRODUCTION MANAGER ....Charles Woolstenhulme

DIRECTOR ....Rouben Mamoulian

ASSISTANT DIRECTOR ....Robert Lee

SCRIPT ....Wallace Smith. Based on an original story
                          by Leo Birinski

DIRECTOR OF PHOTOGRAPHY ..Lucien Andriot

EDITOR ....Margaret Clancey

ART DIRECTOR . . . . Richard Day
MUSICAL DIRECTOR . . . . Alfred Newman
SONGS
'The World is Mine Tonight' . . . George Posford, Holt Marwell; sung by
                                  Nino Martini
'Celeste Aida' . . . . Giuseppe Verdi; sung by Nino Martini
'Adios Mi Terra' . . . . Miguel Sandoval; sung by Nino Martini
Also: 'Cielito Lindo', 'Lamento Gitano', 'Estrellita'
COSTUMES . . . . Omar Kiam
SOUND . . . . Paul Neal

Ida Lupino (Jane), Nino Martini (Chivo), Leo Carrillo (Pablo Braganza),
Harold Huber (Campo), Mischa Auer (Diego), Stanley Fields (Butch), James
Blakeley (Bill), Paul Hurst (American Detective), Adrian Rosley (Radio
Station Manager), Alan Garcia (Police Captain), Frank Puglia (Lopez),
Michael Visaroff (Theatre Manager), Chris-Pin Martin (Pancho), Harry
Semels (Manuel), George Du Count (Salvador), Alphonso Pedroya (Coloso),
Len Brixton (Nick), Trovadores Chinacos (Guitar Trio), M. Alvarez Maciste
(Guitar Soloist).

Released in US, 2 October 1936; UK, 29 November 1936.
Running time: 88 mins.
DISTRIBUTORS United Artists.

High, Wide and Handsome (1937)
PRODUCTION COMPANY . . . . . . Paramount
PRODUCER . . . . Arthur Hornblow, Jr
DIRECTOR . . . . Rouben Mamoulian
ASSISTANT DIRECTOR . . . . Joe Youngerman
SCRIPT . . . . Oscar Hammerstein II
ADDITIONAL DIALOGUE . . . . George O'Neill
DIRECTORS OF PHOTOGRAPHY . Victor Milner, Theodor Sparkuhl
SPECIAL EFFECTS . . . . Gordon Jennings
EDITOR . . . . Archie Marshek

ART DIRECTORS . . . . .Hans Dreier, John Goodman
SET DECORATOR . . . . .A. E. Freudeman
MUSIC .Jerome Kern
MUSICAL DIRECTOR . . . . .Boris Morros
ORCHESTRATIONS . . . . .Robert Russell Bennett
SONGS .Jerome Kern, Oscar Hammerstein II
'High, Wide and Handsome' . . .Sung by Irene Dunne
'Can I Forget You?' . . . . .Sung by Irene Dunne
'The Things I Want' . . . . .Sung by Dorothy Lamour
'Allegheny Al' . . . . .Sung by Irene Dunne and Dorothy Lamour
'Will You Marry Me
Tomorrow, Maria?' . . . . .Sung by William Frawley
'The Folks Who Live on
the Hill' . . . . .Sung by Irene Dunne
COSTUMES . . . . .Travis Banton
CHOREOGRAPHY . . . . .LeRoy Prinz
SOUND . . . . .Charles Hisserich, Don Johnson
TECHNICAL ADVISER . . . . .William Gilmore Beymer

Irene Dunne (Sally Watterson), Randolph Scott (Peter Cortlandt), Dorothy
Lamour (Molly Fuller), Raymond Walburn (Doc Watterson), Alan Hale
(Walter Brennan), Elizabeth Patterson (Grandma Cortlandt), Charles Bickford
(Red Scanlon), William Frawley (Mac), Akim Tamiroff (Joe Varese), Ben Blue
(Samuel), Irving Pichel (Stark), Lucien Littlefield (Dr Lippincott), Helen
Lowell (Mrs Lippincott), Roger Imhof (Pop Bowers), Purnell Pratt (Colonel
Blake), Edward Gargan (Foreman), Tommy Bupp (Boy), Russell Hopton
(John Thompson), Billy Bletcher (Shorty), Stanley Andrews (Lem Moulton),
Frank Sully (Gabby Johnson), Jack Clifford (Walsh Miller), James Burke
(Stackpole), Claire MacDowell (Seamstress), Connie Bergen.

Filmed in the Paramount Studios, and on location at Chino, California,
January–May 1937.
Released in US, 1 October 1937; UK, 18 August 1937. Running time: 111 mins.
DISTRIBUTORS Paramount.

Golden Boy (1939)

PRODUCTION COMPANY	Columbia
PRODUCER	William Perlberg
DIRECTOR	Rouben Mamoulian
ASSISTANT DIRECTOR	Eugene Anderson
SCRIPT	Lewis Meltzer, Daniel Taradash, Sarah Y. Mason, Victor Heerman. Based on the play by Clifford Odets
DIRECTORS OF PHOTOGRAPHY	Nick Musuraca, Karl Freund
EDITOR	Otto Meyer
MONTAGE EFFECTS	Donald W. Starling
ART DIRECTOR	Lionel Banks
MUSIC	Victor Young
MUSICAL DIRECTOR	Morris W. Stoloff
ORCHESTRATIONS	Leo Shuken
SOUND	George Cooper

Barbara Stanwyck (Lorna Moon), Adolphe Menjou (Tom Moody), William Holden (Joe Bonaparte), Lee J. Cobb (Mr Bonaparte), Joseph Calleia (Eddie Fuseli), Sam Levene (Siggie), Edward S. Brophy (Roxy Lewis), Beatrice Blinn (Anna), William H. Strauss (Mr Carp), Don Beddoe (Borneo), Frank Jenks (Boxer), Charles Halton (Newspaperman), John Wray, Clinton Rosemond.

Filmed in the Columbia Studios, Hollywood, April–June 1939.
Released in US, 5 August 1939; UK, 24 November 1939. Running time: 99 mins.
DISTRIBUTORS Columbia.

The Mark of Zorro (1940)

PRODUCTION COMPANY	20th Century-Fox
PRODUCER	Raymond Griffith
DIRECTOR	Rouben Mamoulian
ASSISTANT DIRECTOR	Sidney Bowen
SCRIPT	John Tainton Foote. Based on the novel *The Curse of Capistrano* by Johnston McCulley

ADAPTATION ....Garrett Fort, Bess Meredyth
DIRECTOR OF PHOTOGRAPHY . .Arthur Miller
EDITOR ....Robert Bischoff
ART DIRECTORS ....Richard Day, Joseph C. Wright
SET DECORATOR ....Thomas Little
MUSIC ....Alfred Newman
COSTUMES ....Travis Banton
SOUND ....W. D. Flick, Roger Heman

Tyrone Power (Diego), Linda Darnell (Lolita Quintero), Basil Rathbone (Captain Esteban Pasquale), Gale Sondergaard (Inez Quintero), Eugene Pallette (Father Felipe), J. Edward Bromberg (Don Luis Quintero), Montagu Love (Don Alejandro Vega), Janet Beecher (Senora Isabella Vega), Robert Lowery (Rodrigo), Chris-Pin Martin (Turnkey), George Regas (Sergeant Gonzales), Belle Mitchell (Maria), John Bleifer (Pedro), Frank Puglia (Café Proprietor), Eugen Borden (Officer of the Day), Pedro de Cordoba (Don Miguel), Guy d'Ennery (Don José), Ralph Byrd.

Filmed in the 20th Century-Fox Studios, Hollywood, under the title of *The Californian*, July–September 1940.
Released in US, 8 November 1940; UK, 3 February 1941. Running time: 93 mins.
DISTRIBUTORS 20th Century-Fox.

Blood and Sand (1941)
PRODUCTION COMPANY ......20th Century-Fox
PRODUCER ....Darryl F. Zanuck
ASSOCIATE PRODUCER ....Robert T. Kane
DIRECTOR ....Rouben Mamoulian
ASSISTANT DIRECTORS ....Robert Webb, Sidney Bowen, Henry
            Weinberger
SCRIPT ....Jo Swerling. Based on the novel *Sangre y Arena* by Vicente Blasco Ibañez
DIRECTORS OF PHOTOGRAPHY .Ernest Palmer, Ray Rennahan
COLOUR PROCESS ....Technicolor

TECHNICOLOR DIRECTOR . . . . .Natalie Kalmus
ASSOCIATE TECHNICOLOR
DIRECTOR . . . . .Morgan Padelford
EDITOR . . . . .Robert Bischoff
ART DIRECTORS . . . . .Richard Day, Joseph C. Wright
SET DECORATOR . . . . .Thomas Little
GIPSY THEME MUSIC . . . .'Romance de Amor' by Vicente Gomez
MUSICAL DIRECTOR . . . . .Alfred Newman
COSTUMES . . . . .Travis Banton
TOREADOR COSTUMES . . . . . . .José Dolores Perez Martinez
CHOREOGRAPHY . . . . .Fiesta scenes devised by Hermes Pan; the
                                dance 'El Torero' conceived by Oscar
                                [Budd] Boetticher, executed by Geneva
                                Sawyer
SOUND . . . . .W. D. Flick, Roger Heman

Tyrone Power (Juan Gallardo), Linda Darnell (Carmen Espinosa), Rita
Hayworth (Doña Sol), Nazimova (Señora Augustias), Anthony Quinn
(Manolo de Palma), J. Carrol Naish (Garabato), John Carradine (Nacional),
Laird Cregar (Natalio Curro), Lynn Bari (Encarnacion), Vicente Gomez
(Guitarist), William Montague [Monty Banks] (Antonio Lopez), George
Reeves (Captain Pierre Lauren), Pedro de Cordoba (Don José Alvarez),
Fortunio Bonanova (Pedro Espinosa), Victor Kilian (Priest), Michael Morris
(La Pulga), Charles Stevens (Pablo Gomez), Ann Todd (Carmen as a child),
Cora Sue Collins (Encarnacion as a child), Russell Hicks (Marquis), Maurice
Cass (El Milquetoast), Rex Downing (Juan as a child), John Wallace
(Francisco), Jacqueline Dalya (Gachi), Cullen Johnson (Manolo as a child),
Larry Harris (Pablo as a child), Ted Frye (La Pulga as a child), Schuyler
Standish (Nacional as a child).

Filmed in the 20th Century-Fox Studios, Hollywood, and on location in
Mexico City, January–March 1941.
Released in US, 30 May 1941; UK, 26 January 1942. Running time: 124 mins.
DISTRIBUTORS 20th Century-Fox.

Rings on Her Fingers (1942)

PRODUCTION COMPANY . . . . . .20th Century-Fox
PRODUCER . . . . .Milton Sperling
DIRECTOR . . . . .Rouben Mamoulian
ASSISTANT DIRECTOR . . . . .Gene Bryant
SCRIPT .Ken Englund
STORY .Robert Pirosh, Joseph Schrank
DIRECTOR OF PHOTOGRAPHY . .George Barnes
EDITOR . . . . .Barbara McLean
ART DIRECTORS . . . . .Richard Day, Albert Hogsett
SET DECORATOR . . . . .Thomas Little
MUSICAL DIRECTOR . . . . .Cyril J. Mockridge
SONG
'The Moon Looked
the Other Way' . . . . .Alfred Newman
COSTUMES . . . . .Gwen Wakeling
SOUND .Joseph E. Aiken, Roger Heman

Henry Fonda (John Wheeler), Gene Tierney (Susan Miller), Spring Byington (May Worthington), Laird Cregar (Warren), John Shepperd (Tod Fenwick), Frank Orth (Kellogg, the Private Eye), Henry Stephenson (Colonel Prentiss), Marjorie Gateson (Mrs Fenwick), George Lessey (Mr Fenwick), Iris Adrian (Peggy), Harry Hayden (Train Conductor), Gwendolyn Logan (Miss Callahan), Eric Wilton (Butler), Billy Benedict (Newsboy), Sarah Edwards (Mrs Clancy), Thurston Hall (Mr Beasley), Clara Blandick (Mrs Beasley), Charles Wilson (Captain Hurley), Edgar Norton (Paul), George Lloyd (Chick), Kathryn Sheldon (Landlady), Frank Sully (Taxi driver), Mel Ruick (Roulette Dealer), Mary Treen.

Filmed in the 20th Century-Fox Studios, Hollywood, November 1941–January 1942.
Released in US, 20 March 1942; UK, 12 October 1942.
Running time: 86 mins.
DISTRIBUTORS 20th Century-Fox.

Summer Holiday (1947)

PRODUCTION COMPANY . . . . . .MGM
PRODUCER . . . . .Arthur Freed
PRODUCTION MANAGER . . . . . . .Hugh Boswell
DIRECTOR . . . . .Rouben Mamoulian
ASSISTANT DIRECTOR . . . . .Wallace Worsley
SCRIPT .Frances Goodrich, Albert Hackett. Based on
the play *Ah! Wilderness* by Eugene O'Neill
SCRIPT SUPERVISOR . . . . .Les Martinson
ADAPTATION . . . . .Irving Brecher, Jean Holloway
DIRECTOR OF PHOTOGRAPHY . .Charles Schoenbaum
COLOUR PROCESS . . . . .Technicolor
TECHNICOLOR DIRECTOR . . . . .Natalie Kalmus
ASSOCIATE TECHNICOLOR
DIRECTOR . . . . .Henri Jaffa
CAMERA OPERATOR . . . . .John Schmitz
EDITOR . . . . .Albert Akst
ART DIRECTORS . . . . .Cedric Gibbons, Jack Martin Smith
SET DECORATORS . . . . .Edwin B. Willis, Richard Pefferle
MUSIC .Harry Warren
MUSICAL DIRECTOR . . . . .Lennie Hayton
ORCHESTRATIONS . . . . .Conrad Salinger, Sidney Cutner, Robert
Franklyn
SONGS .Harry Warren, Ralph Blane
'It's Our Home Town' . . . . .Sung by Walter Huston, Mickey Rooney,
Gloria De Haven
'Afraid to Fall in Love' . . . . .Sung by Mickey Rooney, Gloria De Haven
'All Hail Danville High' . . . . . . .Sung by cast
'The Stanley Steamer' . . . . .Sung by Mickey Rooney, Gloria De Haven,
Agnes Moorehead, Walter Huston, etc.
'It's Independence Day' . . . . . . .Sung by cast
'Weary Blues' . . . . .Sung by Marilyn Maxwell
'I Think You're the Sweetest
Kid I've Ever Known' . . . . .Sung by Marilyn Maxwell

```
COSTUMES . . . . . . . . . . . . . . . . .Walter Plunkett
COSTUME SUPERVISOR . . . . . . . .Irene
CHOREOGRAPHY  . . . . . . . . . . . .Charles Walters
SOUND . . . . . . . . . . . . . . . . . . . .Douglas Shearer, Frank B. MacKenzie
```

Mickey Rooney (Richard Miller), Gloria De Haven (Muriel McComber),
Walter Huston (Nat Miller), Frank Morgan (Uncle Sid), Butch Jenkins
(Tommy), Marilyn Maxwell (Belle), Agnes Moorehead (Cousin Lily), Selena
Royle (Mrs Miller), Michael Kirby (Arthur Miller), Shirley Johns (Mildred),
Hal Hackett (Wint), Ann Francis (Elsie Rand), John Alexander (Mr
McComber), Virginia Brissac (Miss Hawley), Howard Freeman (Mr
Peabody), Alice MacKenzie (Mrs McComber), Ruth Brady (Crystal).

Filmed in the MGM Studios, Hollywood, June–October 1946.
Released in US, 20 May 1948; UK, 25 October 1948. Running time: 92 mins.
DISTRIBUTORS MGM.

Silk Stockings (1957)

```
PRODUCTION COMP ANY . . . . . .MGM
PRODUCER  . . . . . . . . . . . . . . . .Arthur Freed
DIRECTOR . . . . . . . . . . . . . . . . .Rouben Mamoulian
ASSISTANT DIRECTOR . . . . . . . .Al Jennings
SCRIPT . . . . . . . . . . . . . . . . . . . .Leonard Gershe, Leonard Spiegelgass.
                                    Based on the book of the musical play by
                                    George S. Kaufman, Leueen McGrath, Abe
                                    Burrows, which was based on the film script
                                    by Billy Wilder, Charles Brackett and
                                    Walter Reisch inspired by the story
                                    'Ninotchka' by Melchior Lengyel
DIRECTOR OF PHOTOGRAPHY . .Robert Bronner
COLOUR PROCESS . . . . . . . . . . .Metrocolor
COLOUR CONSULTANT . . . . . . . .Charles K. Hagedon
EDITOR  . . . . . . . . . . . . . . . . . . .Harold F. Kress
ART DIRECTORS  . . . . . . . . . . . .William A. Horning, Randall Duell
```

SET DECORATORS . . . . .Edwin B. Willis, Hugh Hunt
MUSIC .Cole Porter
MUSICAL DIRECTOR . . . . .André Previn
ORCHESTRATIONS . . . . .Conrad Salinger
ADDITIONAL ORCHESTRATIONS Skip Martin, Al Woodbury
SONGS .Cole Porter
'Too Bad' . . . . .Sung by Fred Astaire, Jules Munshin, Peter
Lorre, Joseph Buloff; danced by them with
Betty Utti, Tybee Afra, Barrie Chase
'Paris Loves Lovers' . . . . .Sung by Fred Astaire, Cyd Charisse
'Stereophonic Sound' . . . . .Sung and danced by Fred Astaire, Janis
Paige
'Chemical Reaction' . . . . .Sung by Cyd Charisse
'All of You' . . . . .Sung by Fred Astaire, danced by Astaire and
Cyd Charisse
'Satin and Silk' . . . . .Sung by Janis Paige
'Silk Stockings' . . . . .Danced by Cyd Charisse
'Without Love' . . . . .Sung by Cyd Charisse
'Fated to Be Mated' . . . . .Sung by Fred Astaire, danced by Astaire and
Cyd Charisse
'Josephine' . . . . .Sung by Janis Paige
'Siberia' . . . . .Sung and danced by Jules Munshin, Peter
Lorre, Joseph Buloff
'Red Blues' . . . . .Sung and danced by Cyd Charisse, Jules
Munshin, Peter Lorre, Joseph Buloff, Wim
Sonneveld, etc.
'The Ritz Roll'n Rock' . . . . .Sung and danced by Fred Astaire
COSTUMES . . . . .Helen Rose
CHOREOGRAPHY . . . . .Hermes Pan (all dances with Astaire);
Eugene Loring (all other dances)
SOUND .Dr Wesley C. Miller (Perspecta
Stereophonic Sound)
SOUND RECORDIST . . . . .Conrad Cahn

Fred Astaire (Steve Canfield), Cyd Charisse (Ninotchka), Janis Paige (Peggy Dainton), Peter Lorre (Brankov), Jules Munshin (Bibinski), Joseph Buloff (Ivanov), George Tobias (Commissar), Wim Sonneveld (Peter Ilyitch Boroff), Belita (Dancer), Ivan Triesault (Russian Embassy Official), Betty Utti, Tybee Afra and Barrie Chase (Dancers).

Filmed in the MGM Studios, Hollywood, November 1956–January 1957. Released in US, 19 July 1957; UK, 1 August 1957. Running time: 117 mins. DISTRIBUTORS MGM.

OTHER ASSIGNMENTS

Laura (1944)

Mamoulian prepared a shooting script and pre-rehearsed the cast. Shooting began on 26 April 1944 with Mamoulian as director, Otto Preminger as producer. Disagreements arose, and in mid-May Mamoulian resigned. The film was completed by Preminger, incorporating the footage shot by Mamoulian and using his shooting script.

Gone to Earth (1950)

Directed by Michael Powell. David Selznick, who had acquired the American rights to the film in return for allowing Jennifer Jones to appear in it, sought an injunction to restrain Sir Alexander Korda and London Films from releasing the film, on the grounds that it distorted the novel on which it was based. The injunction was not granted. For the American release, Mamoulian – as a favour to Selznick – re-edited the film to some extent and did two weeks additional shooting in Hollywood with Jennifer Jones, Cyril Cusack and David Farrar. This version was released in the United States in 1952 as *The Wild Heart*.

Porgy and Bess (1959)

Shooting was set to start on 2 July 1958 with Mamoulian (who had prepared a complete shooting script) as director, but the sets were razed by a fire at Goldwyn Studios. The new start was scheduled for 27 August, but disagreements had arisen between Mamoulian and Goldwyn, and on 27 July

Mamoulian was fired. When shooting finally did start on 22 September, Otto Preminger was the director.

Cleopatra (1963)

Mamoulian was signed as director on 21 October 1959. After a year of preparation, shooting began in London on 28 September 1960, and was suspended on 18 November. On 18 January 1961 Mamoulian resigned, and the film was subsequently made in Italy with Joseph L. Mankiewicz as writer and director. Some of the ten and a half minutes of film shot by Mamoulian was incorporated in the final version.

STAGE PRODUCTIONS

1922   *The Beating on the Door* by Austin Page (St James's Theatre, London, 6 November)

1923   *Rigoletto* by Giuseppe Verdi (American Opera Co. at Eastman Theatre, Rochester, New York)
Faust by Charles Gounod (American Opera Co. at Eastman Theatre, Rochester, New York)
Carmen by Georges Bizet (American Opera Co. at Eastman Theatre, Rochester, New York)

1924   *Boris Godunov* by Modest Mussorgsky (American Opera Co. at Eastman Theatre, Rochester, New York)

1925   *Tannhäuser* by Richard Wagner (American Opera Co. at Eastman Theatre, Rochester, New York)
Pelléas et Mélisande by Claude Debussy (American Opera Co. at Eastman Theatre, Rochester, New York)
Shanewis by Charles Wakefield Cadman (American Opera Co. at Eastman Theatre, Rochester, New York)
The Merry Widow by Franz Lehar (American Opera Co. at Eastman Theatre, Rochester, New York)
The Count of Luxembourg by Franz Lehar (American Opera Co. at Eastman Theatre, Rochester, New York)

H.M.S. Pinafore by Gilbert & Sullivan (American Opera Co. at Eastman Theatre, Rochester, New York)

The Pirates of Penzance by Gilbert & Sullivan (American Opera Co. at Eastman Theatre, Rochester, New York)

Sister Beatrice by Otto Luning (American Opera Co. at Eastman Theatre, Rochester, New York)

1926 *Clarence* by Booth Tarkington (Theatre Guild School, Scarborough, New York)

Enter Madame by Gilda Varesi Archibald and Dorothea Donn Byrne (Theatre Guild School, Scarborough, New York)

He Who Gets Slapped by Leonid Andreyev (Theatre Guild School, Scarborough, New York)

1927 *Seven Keys to Baldpate* by George M. Cohan (Garrick Theatre, London, 3 May, matinée performances)

Porgy by Dorothy and Du Bose Heyward (Guild Theatre, New York, 10 October, 367 performances)

1928 *Marco Millions* by Eugene O'Neill (Guild Theatre, New York, 9 January, 102 performances)

These Modern Women by Lawrence Langner (Eltinge Theatre, New York, 13 February, 24 performances)

Café Tomaza by William Dubois (pre-Broadway tryout, Cort Theatre, Jamaica, New York, 20 April)

Women by Edith and Edward Ellis (pre-Broadway tryout, Adelphi Theatre, Philadelphia, so September)

Congai by Harry Harvey and Carlton Hindreth (Sam H. Harris Theatre, New York, 27 November, 137 performances)

Wings Over Europe by Robert Nichols and Maurice Browne (Martin Beck Theatre, New York, 10 December, 33 performances)

1929 *The Game of Love and Death* by Romain Rolland (Guild Theatre, New York, 25 November, 48 performances)

1930 *R.U.R.* by Karel Čapek (Martin Beck Theatre, New York, 17 February, 16 performances)

A Month in the Country by Ivan Turgenev, adapt. Mamoulian (Guild Theatre, New York, 17 March, 72 performances)

Die glückliche Hand [*The Hand of Fate*] by Arnold Schönberg (Metropolitan Opera House, New York, 22 April; special performances, also at Philadelphia)

A Farewell to Arms by Lawrence Stallings (National Theatre, New York, 22 September, 24 performances)

Solid South by Lewton Campbell (Lyceum Theatre, New York, 14 October, 23 performances)

1935 *Porgy and Bess* by George Gershwin, Du Bose Heyward and Ira Gershwin (Alvin Theatre, New York, 10 October, 124 performances)

1938 *Porgy and Bess* by George Gershwin, Du Bose Heyward and Ira Gershwin (Philharmonic Auditorium Los Angeles and San Francisco)

1943 *Oklahoma!* by Richard Rodgers and Oscar Hammerstein II (St James's Theatre, New York, 31 March, 2248 performances)

1944 *Sadie Thompson* by Vernon Duke, Howard Dietz and Mamoulian (Alvin Theatre, New York, 16 November, 60 performances)

1945 *Carousel* by Richard Rodgers and Oscar Hammerstein II (Majestic Theatre, New York, 19 April, 890 performances)

1946 *St Louis Woman* by Harold Arlen, Johnny Mercer, A. Bontemps and C. Cullen (Martin Beck Theatre, New York, 30 March, 113 performances)

1947 *Oklahoma!* by Richard Rodgers and Oscar Hammerstein II (Drury Lane, London, 30 April, 1543 performances)

1949 *Leaf and Bough* by Joseph Hayes (Cort Theatre, Jamaica, New York, 21 January, 3 performances)

Lost in the Stars by Kurt Weill and Maxwell Anderson (Music Box Theatre, 30 October, 281 performances)

1950 *Arms and the Girl* by Morton Gould, Mamoulian, Herbert and Dorothy Fields (46th Street Theatre, New York, 2 February, 134 performances)

Carousel by Richard Rodgers and Oscar Hammerstein II (Drury Lane, London, 7 June, 566 performances)

1951 *Oklahoma!* by Richard Rodgers and Oscar Hammerstein II (Broadway Theatre, New York, 29 May, 72 performances; and Berlin Art Festival in September)

1953 Adolph Zukor's Golden Jubilee (Palladium, Hollywood, in May)

1954 *Carousel* by Richard Rodgers and Oscar Hammerstein II (Civic Light Opera Co., Los Angeles and San Francisco)

1955 *Oklahoma!* by Richard Rodgers and Oscar Hammerstein II (for 'Salute to France' programme sponsored by A.N.T.A. and American State Department, at Paris, Rome, Milan, Naples, Venice, in May)

1966 *Shakespeare's Hamlet, A New Version* by Rouben Mamoulian (Garrick Theatre, Transylvania College, University of Kentucky)

In collaboration with Maxwell Anderson, Mamoulian wrote (c. 1952–3) adaptations of *Carmen* and *The Barber of Seville*; a play, *The Devil's Hornpipe*, also written in collaboration with Maxwell Anderson, was filmed in 1958 as *Never Steal Anything Small* (script and direction, Charles Lederer). Mamoulian has published two books: *Abigayil*, a children's story (1964) and *Hamlet Revised and Interpreted* (1965). Among several periodical articles: 'Some Problems in the Direction of Colour Pictures' (in *International Photographer*, July 1935); 'Bernhardt versus Duse' (in *Theatre Arts*, September 1957)

Acknowledgments

For the quotations from Mamoulian in this book, I have plundered three interviews: with Jean Douchet and Bertrand Tavernier in *Positif* no. 64/65, 1964; with Andrew Sarris in *Interviews with Film Directors*, Bobbs-Merrill, 1967; and above all, with David Robinson in *Sight and Sound*, Summer 1961 – still the best, most attractive and most informative interview with Mamoulian to have been published.

Stills are by courtesy of Paramount, MGM, Samuel Goldwyn/United Artists, Pickford-Lasky, Columbia, 20th Century-Fox and the National Film Archive. Personally, I am indebted for help, advice and patient forbearance to a great many people; in particular to David Meeker, Philip Jenkinson, Gillian Hartnoll, Sheila Whitaker, Paul Willemen, Jan Dawson, Sylvia Loeb, Richard Roud, Penelope Houston, Carol Fleming and Jo Wimshurst.

List of Illustrations

Index

Page numbers in **bold** indicate detailed analysis; those in *italic* denote illustrations. *n* = endnote.